Getting Started with SpriteKit

Develop fun and exciting games and create amazing animations for your existing apps with SpriteKit, Apple's 2D game development framework

Jorge Jordán

[PACKT] open source*
PUBLISHING
community experience distilled

BIRMINGHAM - MUMBAI

Getting Started with SpriteKit

First published: January 2016

Production reference: 1200116

Published by Packt Publishing Ltd.
Livery Place
35 Livery Street
Birmingham B3 2PB, UK.

ISBN 978-1-78588-733-8

www.packtpub.com

Credits

Author
Jorge Jordán

Reviewer
Andrew Kenady

Commissioning Editor
Amarabha Banerjee

Acquisition Editor
Prachi Bisht

Content Development Editor
Arshiya Ayaz Umer

Technical Editor
Vishal Mewada

Copy Editor
Vedangi Narvekar

Project Coordinator
Shipra Chawhan

Proofreader
Safis Editing

Indexer
Priya Sane

Graphics
Kirk D'Penha

Production Coordinator
Shantanu N. Zagade

Cover Work
Shantanu N. Zagade

About the Author

Jorge Jordán is an iOS indie developer who's passionate about how things work since his childhood. This is the reason why he graduated in computer science and became a Java developer. After buying his first iPhone, he became deeply interested in its technology and spent his spare time learning how to develop apps for Apple's smartphones.

Over time, he founded www.insaneplatypusgames.com, where he tries to make his dreams and games come true. He is also a member of the tutorial team at www.raywenderlich.com.

Also, he has worked on a book titled *Cocos2d Game Development Blueprints*, *Packt Publishing*.

In his free time, he loves to play video games, play bass guitar, and watch TV series.

You can follow him on Twitter; his Twitter handle is @jjordanarenas.

I would like to thank my family, especially my mom and brother, for always believing in me. Thanks to them, I am the person that I am. I would also like to thank the people who have encouraged me unconditionally, especially Angélica, for being so patient and for her support while I was writing this book.

Thanks to José Antonio Espino (joseantonio.espinosuar@gmail.com) for creating all the art for this book and designing these amazing characters and content.

Also, thanks to all my friends: the canupis (especially to you, Eugenio, wherever you are), Javi Sáez, Kike, Pedro, Fanny, Guille, and Carmelo for all the laughs and the good times that we spend together.

I finally want to thank all the people from Packt Publishing for their efforts to make this book real.

About the Reviewer

Andrew Kenady is a game engineer from Kentucky. He holds a bachelor's degree in computer science from Western Kentucky University and has worked professionally in the games industry since his graduation in 2013. His published titles span multiple genres and platforms and include Battlepillars and Draw a Stickman: EPIC 2. He is currently working for NC2 Media, a Tennessee-based tech company, on new and promising confidential products for the mobile games sector.

In addition to working on this publication, Andrew has worked in the past as a reviewer for *iOS Game Programming Cookbook* by *Bhanu Birani* and *Chhavi Vaishnav*.

www.PacktPub.com

Support files, eBooks, discount offers, and more

For support files and downloads related to your book, please visit www.PacktPub.com.

Did you know that Packt offers eBook versions of every book published, with PDF and ePub files available? You can upgrade to the eBook version at www.PacktPub.com and as a print book customer, you are entitled to a discount on the eBook copy. Get in touch with us at service@packtpub.com for more details.

At www.PacktPub.com, you can also read a collection of free technical articles, sign up for a range of free newsletters and receive exclusive discounts and offers on Packt books and eBooks.

https://www2.packtpub.com/books/subscription/packtlib

Do you need instant solutions to your IT questions? PacktLib is Packt's online digital book library. Here, you can search, access, and read Packt's entire library of books.

Why subscribe?

- Fully searchable across every book published by Packt
- Copy and paste, print, and bookmark content
- On demand and accessible via a web browser

Free access for Packt account holders

If you have an account with Packt at www.PacktPub.com, you can use this to access PacktLib today and view 9 entirely free books. Simply use your login credentials for immediate access.

Table of Contents

Preface

I think that I'm not wrong if I say that we as developers have the healthy (or unhealthy) habit of trying to decompose mentally (or even physically) everything that comes to our hands into smaller pieces to understand how it works.

In my case, I have to acknowledge that I am a video game lover and a restless developer, and every time I get a game or an app, I can't stop myself from thinking about how an animation or a particular effect is achieved.

This concern helped me learn how to develop apps and games. Thanks to this, I discovered that Apple provides a powerful set of tools that can be combined to create amazing games and stunning apps.

One of these tools is SpriteKit, a 2D game engine that is at the forefront of the frameworks that are available on the market and which can be included in any application to provide its dynamic features.

If you are reading these lines, you probably are either a game lover with a curiosity to learn how video games are developed, or you are an app developer who wants to know how the animations that you have seen in other apps or games have been created.

At this point starts a journey full of new experiences and knowledge that will satisfy all your curiosity. So take a seat, get comfortable, and start reading and enjoying.

What this book covers

This book contains six chapters that will guide you through the process of creating a video game with the tools provided by SpriteKit. At the same time, you will learn how to deal with the common difficulties that you may come across when developing games and how to apply the techniques that you learn here to give a stunning look to an app.

Chapter 1, The First Steps toward SpriteKit, covers the basics of developing a game with SpriteKit. In this chapter, you will learn what a game engine is and what a new SpriteKit project looks like. In addition to this, you will learn the purpose of the SKNode and SKScene classes and how to utilize them to add a background and a sprite into the game.

Chapter 2, What Makes a Game a Game?, shows the main techniques used in game development, such as moving sprites on the scene, detecting touches, and handling collisions. In addition to this, you will learn how to create and update labels and play music and sound effects.

Chapter 3, Taking Games One Step Further, teaches advanced techniques such us how to create complex nodes by extending the SKNode class or implement the parallax effect. You will also learn how to draw geometrical primitives and animate sprites.

Chapter 4, From Basic to Professional Games, helps us provide our game with the needed components to consider it as a finished product. You will learn how to create a Game Over condition for the game and a main menu scene from where you will learn how to transition to a tutorial that you will create for players so that they know the mechanism of the game. You will also learn how to save and load data from internal and external sources.

Chapter 5, Utilizing the Hardware and Graphics Processor, teaches you how to get the most advantage from the hardware of physical devices using the accelerometer or creating stunning visual effects by adding shaders, lights, and shadows into a game.

Chapter 6, Auxiliary Techniques, covers the development of special effects, which are also known as particle systems, and ways to combine SpriteKit with UIKit in order to create robust games and dynamic apps. You will also learn how to use third-party tools to create custom audio and fonts and find resources that can be used in games.

What you need for this book

To follow the implementation of the code provided in this book, you will need the following hardware and software:

- An Intel-based Mac that runs on Mac OS X 10.10.4 or later
- The latest version of Xcode (version 7.0 at the time of writing this book)
- An enrollment in the iOS Developer Program if you want to test the games on a device
- An iOS device to test games on it

You will not need a lot of experience developing with Swift or SpriteKit as the chapters will help you easily understand how to utilize the tools provided by the game development framework.

Who this book is for

If you are an iOS developer who wants to learn which tools offer the game development framework provided by Apple so that you can add an extra edge to your applications or learn how to bring to life the games that you have imagined in your mind, this book is for you. It has been written to teach the key concepts of 2D game development and ways to create 2D games using SpriteKit. This book will help you deploy framework tools to improve the visual experience of your apps.

Conventions

There are several text styles in this book that refer to different type of information. For example, you will find words referring code that will look like the following line:

There are a couple of storyboard files, namely `Main` and `LaunchScreen`, which are responsible for showing the game screen and launch image respectively.

You will find code blocks that look like this:

```
import UIKit

@UIApplicationMain
class AppDelegate: UIResponder, UIApplicationDelegate {

    var window: UIWindow?
```

```
     func application(application: UIApplication,
didFinishLaunchingWithOptions launchOptions: [NSObject: AnyObject]?)
-> Bool {
        // Override point for customization after application launch.
        return true
     }
```

If you are expected to perform some actions on specific places of the screen you will find the instructions highlighted in the following way:

To create a new **SpriteKit** project, we need to open **Xcode** and then navigate to **File | New | Project...**.

You will find instructions specifying the exact value you have to enter in a text field that will look like the following line:

Call it Enemy and choose the folder where you want it to be saved.

Hints, tips, advices and notes will look like this:

> Note that we just need to create a motion manager instance as thanks to it we can retrieve all the motion data we need.

Sometimes you are going to be challenged by me, requesting you to try to solve a particular situation. These challenges will be labeled as 1-star, 2-star or 3-star Challenge depending on the difficulty of the task, but they can be solved with the knowledge acquired along the book:

2-star challenge: colliding puppets

Reader feedback

Feedback from our readers is always welcome. Let us know what you think about this book—what you liked or disliked. Reader feedback is important for us as it helps us develop titles that you will really get the most out of.

To send us general feedback, simply e-mail feedback@packtpub.com, and mention the book's title in the subject of your message.

If there is a topic that you have expertise in and you are interested in either writing or contributing to a book, see our author guide at www.packtpub.com/authors.

Customer support

Now that you are the proud owner of a Packt book, we have a number of things to help you to get the most from your purchase.

Downloading the example code

You can download the example code files from your account at `http://www.packtpub.com` for all the Packt Publishing books you have purchased. If you purchased this book elsewhere, you can visit `http://www.packtpub.com/support` and register to have the files e-mailed directly to you.

Downloading the color images of this book

We also provide you with a PDF file that has color images of the screenshots/diagrams used in this book. The color images will help you better understand the changes in the output. You can download this file from `http://www.packtpub.com/sites/default/files/downloads/GettingStartedWithSpriteKit_ColorImages.pdf`.

Errata

Although we have taken every care to ensure the accuracy of our content, mistakes do happen. If you find a mistake in one of our books—maybe a mistake in the text or the code—we would be grateful if you could report this to us. By doing so, you can save other readers from frustration and help us improve subsequent versions of this book. If you find any errata, please report them by visiting `http://www.packtpub.com/submit-errata`, selecting your book, clicking on the **Errata Submission Form** link, and entering the details of your errata. Once your errata are verified, your submission will be accepted and the errata will be uploaded to our website or added to any list of existing errata under the Errata section of that title.

To view the previously submitted errata, go to `https://www.packtpub.com/books/content/support` and enter the name of the book in the search field. The required information will appear under the **Errata** section.

Piracy

Piracy of copyrighted material on the Internet is an ongoing problem across all media. At Packt, we take the protection of our copyright and licenses very seriously. If you come across any illegal copies of our works in any form on the Internet, please provide us with the location address or website name immediately so that we can pursue a remedy.

Please contact us at copyright@packtpub.com with a link to the suspected pirated material.

We appreciate your help in protecting our authors and our ability to bring you valuable content.

Questions

If you have a problem with any aspect of this book, you can contact us at questions@packtpub.com, and we will do our best to address the problem.

1
The First Step toward SpriteKit

In 2013, Apple released SpriteKit, its 2D game engine, in order to compete with all the two-dimensional frameworks that were existing in the market and retain their developers in its own technological ecosystem. Since then, SpriteKit has become one of the most powerful tools that are used to develop 2D games for iOS. In this chapter, we will have a look at the elements that are a part of game development, and we'll study how to use them with SpriteKit.

In this chapter, we will explore the following topics:

- Understanding game engines
- Creating and understanding a new SpriteKit project
- Understanding the SKNode class
- Studying the SKScene class
- How to add a sprite and background to a scene

Game engines

I remember the time when I developed my first game using the BASIC programming language on my old Amstrad CPC. In those times, every game was hardware-specific, which means that you had to take into account every machine's low-level characteristics.

A game engine is a collection of software instructions that eases the process of game development by providing abstraction between the hardware and software layers. This way, you don't need to waste your efforts when performing important tasks, such as handling user inputs, playing sound and video, rendering images, or simulating physics.

As mentioned previously, SpriteKit is an engine developed by Apple to create games, and it's one of the most powerful tools that are used to build native 2D games for both iOS and Max OS X.

Creating a new SpriteKit project

The tool needed to develop SpriteKit games is Apple's **Integrated Development Environment (IDE)** Xcode, which can be found free of charge on Apple's App Store at `https://itunes.apple.com/en/app/xcode/id497799835?l=en&mt=12`. We are going to work with version 7.0, which is the latest at the time of writing the book, and iOS 9.

Creating a new project with Xcode is a straightforward task, but I would like to take advantage of it to help you understand how a default Xcode project looks like.

To create a new SpriteKit project, we need to open **Xcode** and then navigate to **File | New | Project...**. On the left-hand side, you will need to click on the **iOS | Application Template**; you will see what's shown in the following screenshot:

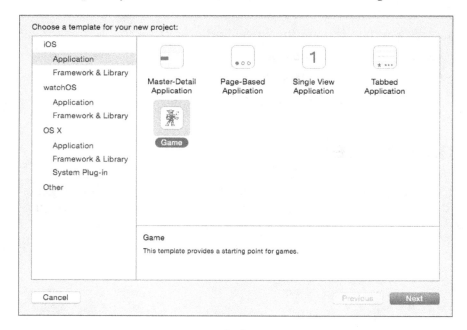

At this point, you will need to perform the following steps:

1. Select the **Game** template and click on **Next**.

2. Set **InsideTheHat** as the template name. Ensure that the **Swift** option is chosen in the **Language** menu. Select **SpriteKit** as the **Game Technology**, and **Universal** is chosen on the **Device Family** menu. Leave the default configuration (checked) for **Include Unit Tests** and **Include UI Tests** before clicking on the **Next** button.

3. Choose a place to save your project in and click on **Create**.

The first thing that you should look at is the left section, which is called **Project Navigator** and contains the folders, and files that will be a part of our game; this section is shown in the following screenshot:

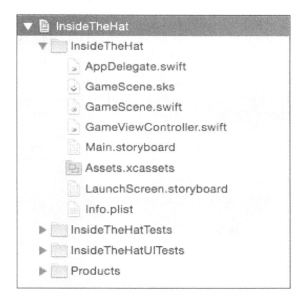

The **Project Navigator** shows a tree of files and folders that represents a hierarchy that doesn't correspond with how these files are located on your hard drive. It means that, if you move some file, on the **Project Navigator**, it won't affect their position in **Finder**. However, if you move some file in **Finder**, the reference kept by Xcode will be broken and it won't be able to make use of it.

The yellow containers on the project navigator are called **Groups** in Xcode, and they are equivalent to folders in a filesystem; as folders, the groups' responsibility is to organize all the files (images, classes, and so on) of an Xcode project.

One of the most important groups is the one called **Project**. It contains classes and resource files. As you can see in the preceding screenshot, a default project contains three **Swift** classes, namely `AppDelegate`, `GameScene`, and `GameViewController`, that will contain the core of the game.

> Swift is Apple's programming language that was created by Apple for iOS, Mac OS X, watchOS, and Linux development. It was first released in June 2014.

There are a couple of storyboard files, namely `Main` and `LaunchScreen`, that are responsible for showing the game screen and launch image respectively. You will also see an image `asset` file, which will contain the images used on the game, and a `plist` file with the project configuration.

In addition to this, there is a file called `GameScene.sks` that should look pretty new to you. This file is used to build the screen in a static way, which is similar to a storyboard, that is created with **Interface Builder**.

Getting back to Xcode, there is another important section in the **Project**; it is the window at the center, which shows the configuration of the **Project**, as shown in the following screenshot:

In this panel, you will see three different sections, namely **Identity**, **Deployment Info**, and **App Icons and Launch Images**. Let's take a look at the second one first, where you can configure the following:

- **Deployment Target**: This is the iOS version that is used to run the game. By default, 9.0 is chosen.

- **Devices**: This is the family of devices (iPhone, iPad, or both), on which we will be able to run the game. In our case, it shows **Universal**, which is the property that we specified when creating the project.

- **Main Interface**: This is the main storyboard file that is used to run the project.

- **Device Orientation**: This determines the different orientations that our game will be able to support. As we are going to develop a vertical game, unselect the **Landscape Left** and **Landscape Right** checkboxes, leaving just **Portrait** checked off.

- **Status Bar Style**: This helps us determine how we want the status bar to be shown.

The third section contains the following configuration:

- **App Icons Source**: This comprises the asset catalog for app icons.

- **Launch Images Source**: This comprises the asset catalog for the launch image.

- **Launch Screen File**: This determines the screen shown while loading the game. If you want to avoid the launch screen that shows the copyright (such as the one that you can use to show your company's logo), choose **Main. Storyboard** in the drop-down menu.

After performing the aforementioned modifications, the project's properties will meet our requirements. So, let's run the project.

Running the project for first time

To execute the project, you just need to click on the **Run** icon at the top left of the **Xcode** screen, and it will run the project on an **iPhone 6** on the **iOS Simulator**; the result is shown in the following screenshot:

Well, with a little effort, we have created our first **Hello, World** project using SpriteKit. Now, it's time to look at the code and understand why the preceding screenshot is the result of these files.

From now on, we are going to assume that we are running the game on the iOS Simulator.

How the default project looks like

In this section, you are not supposed to understand everything. The aim of this section is to understand the responsibility of each class in a default SpriteKit project.

The entry point of our game is the AppDelegate class, which is the same as that of all iOS applications. Let's take a look at its content:

```
import UIKit

@UIApplicationMain
class AppDelegate: UIResponder, UIApplicationDelegate {

    var window: UIWindow?

    func application(application: UIApplication,
didFinishLaunchingWithOptions launchOptions: [NSObject: AnyObject]?)
-> Bool {
        // Override point for customization after application launch.
        return true
    }
}
```

 Downloading the example code.

You can download the example code files from your account at http://www.packtpub.com for all the Packt Publishing books you have purchased. If you purchased this book elsewhere, you can visit http://www.packtpub.com/support and register to have the files e-mailed directly to you.

I've just pasted the top block of the file because it is the important one. As you can see, we imported the UIKit framework that will provide the window and the view architecture needed to build an application. It also provides our project with the event-handling infrastructure that is needed to respond to user input and the app model needed to drive the main run loop and interact with the system.

The next line contains an odd-looking instruction, which is @UIApplicationMain. This tells Xcode which is the main file of the project.

Then, you will see that the `AppDelegate` class inherits from `UIResponder` and `UIApplicationDelegate`, which is what happens with all iOS applications. We declared a `UIWindow` optional variable to avoid runtime errors in case of nil content.

 As per Apple's documentation (`https://developer.apple.com/library/mac/documentation/Swift/Conceptual/Swift_Programming_Language/OptionalChaining.html`), **optional chaining** is a Swift process that is used to call properties and methods on an optional that might currently be `nil`. If the optional contains a value, the call succeeds, and if the optional is `nil`, the call returns `nil`.

Finally, you will see that the only method implemented is `application(application:, launchOptions:)`. This is the point where we can apply some instructions that we want the game to execute as soon as it's launched.

There is nothing more to remark on this class. So let's take a look at the class that will be called just after `AppDelegate`: `GameViewController`.

To understand why this class is called, as soon as the main screen is launched, we need to keep in mind that the project is configured to show `Main.storyboard` as the main interface. In the **Project Explorer**, select the **File** and look at the **Utilities** panel on the right-hand side of screen, and choose the **Identity Inspector** to have a look at its configuration, as shown in the following screenshot:

This means that the interface is linked to the `GameViewController` class. It's time to open the class and discover what it contains:

```
import UIKit
import SpriteKit

class GameViewController: UIViewController {
override func viewDidLoad() {
        super.viewDidLoad()
```

```
if let scene = GameScene(fileNamed:"GameScene") {
    // Configure the view.
    let skView = self.view as! SKView
    skView.showsFPS = true
    skView.showsNodeCount = true

    /* Sprite Kit applies additional optimizations to improve
rendering performance */
    skView.ignoresSiblingOrder = true

    /* Set the scale mode to scale to fit the window */
    scene.scaleMode = .AspectFill

    skView.presentScene(scene)
    }
}
```

As you can see at the top of the file, the view controller is a subclass of the UIViewController class, which is commonly seen in many iOS applications. However, the difference is that here, we imported the SpriteKit framework (apart from UIKit), to provide game characteristics to the project.

This class overrides the viewDidLoad method, where we create a scene by using a file called GameScene. This file corresponds to GameScene.sks. If it succeeds, we create a view (an instance of the SKView class), setting the showsFPS and showsNodeCount attributes to True.

This is the reason why we can see these labels at the bottom right of the game's screen; they show the amount of draw calls (node count), and frame rate respectively.

 The frame rate value measures how smooth our game will be. In iOS, the maximum frame rate is 60 Hz.

The number of draw calls and the frame rate are values that you need to take care of, as they will let us know if our game will run smoothly.

We will have a look at the last view's configuration (ignoresSiblingOrder), and the scaleMode property later in the chapter, as we just want to have an overview the project. Once the view is configured, we can load the scene by calling the presentScene method.

Next, in the file, you will see four more methods. Take a look at the following two methods:

```
override func shouldAutorotate() -> Bool {
    return true
}

override func supportedInterfaceOrientations() ->
UIInterfaceOrientationMask {
    if UIDevice.currentDevice().userInterfaceIdiom == .Phone {
        return .AllButUpsideDown
    } else {
        return .All
    }
}
```

This code means that the user can rotate the device, and the screen will adapt itself automatically to the new orientation with one restriction, due to the AllButUpsideDown property: the game's screen won't rotate when we hold the iPhone or iPod devices upside down.

Have a look at the following method:

```
override func didReceiveMemoryWarning() {
    super.didReceiveMemoryWarning()
    // Release any cached data, images, etc that aren't in use.
}
```

This method should look familiar to you if you have developed an iOS application previously. It's raised by the system when the amount of available memory is low. It allows us to release some memory to avoid an application crash.

Finally, we have the following method that has to do with the way the game is shown:

```
override func prefersStatusBarHidden() -> Bool {
    return true
}
```

This method keeps the status bar hidden, as our application is a game and we want to use the full screen to show it.

We have previously seen that this class creates a scene by calling the constructor method in the GameScene class. Therefore, it's time to open the file:

```
import SpriteKit

class GameScene: SKScene {
    override func didMoveToView(view: SKView) {
        /* Setup your scene here */
        let myLabel = SKLabelNode(fontNamed:"Chalkduster")
        myLabel.text = "Hello, World!";
        myLabel.fontSize = 65;
        myLabel.position = CGPoint(x:CGRectGetMidX(self.frame),
y:CGRectGetMidY(self.frame));

        self.addChild(myLabel)
    }
```

As you can see, this class also imports the SpriteKit framework, but the most important thing about this is the class that it is inheriting SKScene. We will study it in detail further in this chapter, but for now, you need to understand that an instance of SKScene or its subclass is the object that will represent a scene of content in a SpriteKit game.

The didMoveToView method means that its code will be executed as soon as the scene is presented by a view. This is the perfect place to initialize a scene and, as we can see, in the default project, we are creating a new label using a font called Chalkduster and configuring some of its properties to set the size, text, and desired position. Adding the label to the scene is as easy as executing the addChild method.

The next method in the class looks like this:

```
    override func touchesBegan(touches: Set<UITouch>, withEvent event:
UIEvent?) {
        /* Called when a touch begins */

        for touch in touches {
            let location = touch.locationInNode(self)

            let sprite = SKSpriteNode(imageNamed:"Spaceship")

            sprite.xScale = 0.5
            sprite.yScale = 0.5
            sprite.position = location
```

```
            let action = SKAction.rotateByAngle(CGFloat(M_PI),
    duration:1)

            sprite.runAction(SKAction.repeatActionForever(action))

            self.addChild(sprite)
        }
    }
```

This method is called when the user touches somewhere on the screen. It is also one of the methods that we can override to handle touches. There are three more methods, namely touchesMoved, touchesEnded, and touchesCancelled, which will be covered in detail in *Chapter 2, What Makes a Game a Game?* As soon as user touches on the screen and this whole process gets completed, it gets the location of the touch, creates an SKSpriteNode instance using the Spaceship texture, sets its size to half of the texture's original size, and places it on the touch position. You will find the image that is used to create the spaceship in the Assets.xcassets folder of the **Project Navigator**.

Then, it applies a rotation to the spaceship by creating an action method, and calling the rotateByAngle method, which accepts an angle value as an input parameter, and running this action on the spaceship. Finally, it adds the ship to the scene.

The SKSpriteNode instance is one of the most used classes in SpriteKit game development as it provides a visual representation and a physical shape to the objects in view.

The last method looks like this:

```
override func update(currentTime: CFTimeInterval) {
    /* Called before each frame is rendered */
}
```

This is one of the most important methods when developing games with SpriteKit, as it is called just before each frame is rendered and it is the place where we can perform important operations and actions.

If you run the project again and touch anywhere on the screen, you will see something that is similar to what's shown in the following screenshot:

As expected, a spaceship has been created and it has begun to rotate in a counterclockwise direction. Another important thing to note at this point is the number of nodes, which has increased and corresponds to the draw of the scene, the text label, the spaceship, and the background.

Now that we had an overview of the initial project code, it's time to go deeper into some of the classes that we saw earlier. We have seen that the default project creates instances of SKScene, SKLabelNode, and SKSpriteNode, which are subclasses of SKNode, one of the most important classes of the SpriteKit framework. You will understand why if you keep reading.

The SKNode class

When developing a scene, we sometimes build what is called a scene hierarchy. This **scene graph** is a hierarchy of the **nodes** that are available on it.

We call them nodes because they inherit from the SKNode class. For more information, visit https://developer.apple.com/library/ios/documentation/ SpriteKit/Reference/SKNode_Ref, which is the main SpriteKit class that renders visual elements.

The following diagram corresponds to the scene graph of the project. You can see that there is a parent SKScene node with two children that correspond to the SKSpriteNode and SKLabelNode that we have added to the game:

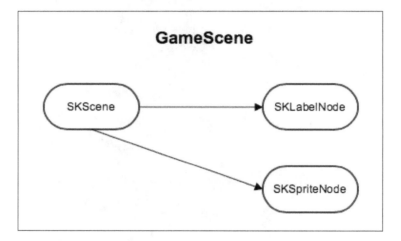

The SKNode class is a subclass of UIResponder. This means that all the SKNode instances and every subclass of SKNode will be able to handle touches and other kind of events such as motion events.

If you look at the SKNode class hierarchy in the following diagram, you will realize the importance of this class, as it is the parent of several useful classes:

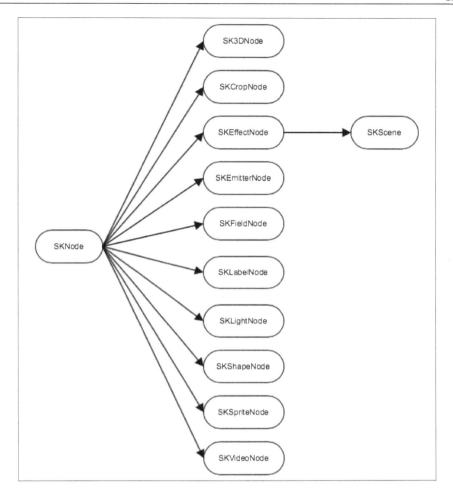

The SKNode class properties

In this section, we are going to have a look at the most important properties available in the SKNode class in detail.

The position property

An important property of nodes is their position, as we are going to manipulate this several times during the game's development. This property corresponds to the position of the node in the parent's coordinate system. Therefore, we need to take it into account when adding new elements to a scene. Its default value is (0.0, 0.0).

The frame property

Another useful property is the frame of a node, which makes a reference to the rectangle defined by its texture (the visual content). This property size can be modified by applying a scaling factor on both the width and height by applying a value between 0 and 1 to the xScale and yScale attributes. The frame can also be rotated by modifying the zRotation property, which will apply a counterclockwise rotation if the value is greater than 0.

 As a node can be used to organize the content by storing other nodes, the scale and rotation modifiers will affect both the node and its descendants.

If we want to take into account a node's descendants when getting its frame, there is a function called calculateAccumulatedFrame() that retrieves the rectangle containing the content of the parent and children while taking into account the scale and rotation factors.

We can, for instance, determine whether this whole frame is intersected by another node's frame thanks to this method.

The zPosition property

This property determines the height of the node related to its parent. Its value is 0.0 by default, but we can set positive or negative values so that, the bigger the zPosition value, the closer the node will be to the user. This way, we will have full control over how the children are rendered.

The hidden property

Sometimes, we will need to keep a node invisible while it is in a scene. We can do this by setting the hidden property to true. It only affects the way the node and its descendants are rendered, as they will still be able to perform actions and collide with other nodes in the scene.

An alpha property

A property that provides a similar effect is the alpha property of the node. It applies a modifier between 0.0 and 1.0 to the alpha component of each pixel and allows us to make the node transparent.

The children node

This read-only array of the `AnyObject` type contains all the node `children` in an `SKNode` object.

name

If a scene contains several nodes, we may need to identify them in order to handle collisions. In such cases, it is a good approach to provide a value to each node's `name` property. We can use this property to give the same name to a group of nodes in order to differentiate them from the player's node and make collision detection tasks easy.

If we want to find a node by its unique name, we can make use of the `childNodeWithName` method. On the other hand, if we have used a name to identify a collection of nodes, we can call `enumerateChildNodesWithName:usingBlock`, which will search a node's children and execute a block of code once for each child that is found.

userInteractionEnabled

There is another property that is commonly used, `userInteractionEnabled`. This determines whether a node can receive touch events. If its value is `false`, the node won't react to user input.

Using SKNode to organize a scene

We have seen previously that an `SKNode` instance can be used to contain other nodes in order to organize the scene content. The following are a few examples:

*   You may want to group several nodes that need to be treated as a unique object to represent an army of alien ships, and you don't want any of the ships to be the root. Grouping them as `children` of a node will allow you to move them, while always keeping the line-up.

- In a game, it is common to have a background, several characters, objects to collide, texts, and many more elements. You can create different layers to separate each of these different kind of elements by creating basic nodes and inserting them in the desired order into the scene.

In the preceding screenshot, you can see how we used three different layers, one for the background, another one for the ninja character, and the last one for the score.

By following the afore mentioned approaches, you will be able to add or remove entire groups of objects by deleting a single node. This will make the scene management more efficient. You can also configure the properties of several nodes by applying the configuration to the root node. You can even take advantage of it when running actions or handling physics contacts.

SKScene

The SKScene class is a subclass of SKNode that has some specific properties and methods to handle the way content is drawn in an SKView object (the screen).

The game loop

Each node provides content that will be animated and rendered by the scene in a process called **game loop**. It looks like the following screenshot that was taken from `https://developer.apple.com/library/ios/documentation/GraphicsAnimation/Conceptual/SpriteKit_PG`:

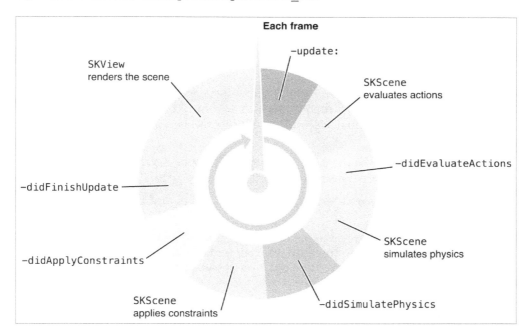

According to the preceding screenshot, each frame in a SpriteKit game is calculated in the following order:

1. Firstly, the `scene` calls the `update` method. Here, we can specify the code that we want to execute just before the scene actions are evaluated.

2. Then, the `scene` executes the actions on its `children` nodes.

3. Once the actions have been executed, the `scene` triggers its `didEvaluateActions` method. We should include in this method the code that we want to execute as soon as the actions have been evaluated.

4. Now, it's time for the physics to be evaluated. SpriteKit provides an easy way to simulate physics in a node such as `gravity`, `collisions`, and `friction`, but we are not going to cover it in this book. You just need to know that there is a step in the game loop where the `scene` executes every physics simulation on the physic bodies in the scene.

5. After the physics is simulated, the scene triggers its `didSimulatePhysics` method. We should include in this method the code that we want to execute as soon as the physics is simulated.

6. Then, the scene applies the constraints associated to its `children` nodes. These constraints are an array of instances of the SKConstraint class, which basically are restrictions applied to a node that can be related to another node in the scene. For example, we can create constraints to set a node's `zRotation` method so that it always points at another node or position in the scene, or keeps a node inside a specified rectangle or within a specified distance of another node.

7. Once the constraints have been applied, the scene triggers its `didApplyConstraints` method, which we should take advantage of to include the code that we want to execute as soon as the physics has been simulated.

8. Then, the scene calls the `didFinishUpdate` method, which is the last method that is called before the scene is rendered.

9. Finally, the scene renders all of its children nodes and updates the view.

 You don't need to call the aforementioned methods directly, because they are called once per frame as long as the scene is presented in the view and it is not paused.

The SKScene properties

In this section, we are going to study in detail the most important properties that are available in the SKScene class.

scaleMode

An SKScene instance provides some properties that can become interesting when creating a scene. For example, the `scaleMode` property allows us to specify the way a scene is mapped to the view that presents it, which can be one of the following four values defined in the SKSceneScaleMode enumeration:

- `Fill`: Each axis of the scene (x and y) is scaled independently. This way, each axis in the scene exactly maps to the length of the same axis in the view.

- `AspectFill`: This is the `scale` mode that is used by the default project. In this case, we will choose a scaling factor, that will be the larger scaling factor between the two dimensions, and each axis of the scene will be scaled by the same factor. This way, the entire area of the view will be filled, but it's possible that some parts of the scene may be cropped.

- AspectFit: In this case, we will choose a scaling factor that will be the smaller scaling factor between the two dimensions, and each axis of the scene will be scaled by the same factor. This way, the entire scene will be visible, but letterboxing may be required in the view.

- ResizeFill: This value will automatically resize the scene so that its dimensions match those of the view.

anchorPoint

This property makes reference to the origin point of the scene. By default, its value is (0,0), which means that the scene will be pinned to the bottom left point of the view, as shown in the following screenshot. When we add the first sprite to the scene, we'll see how important it is:

size

This property specifies the part of the scene's coordinate space that is visible in the view. When this property is changed, the didChangeSize method is triggered. An important aspect that needs to be highlighted is that this property will also be modified if we set the ResizeFill value in the scaleMode property.

backgroundColor

If we are not planning to add a background image to our game, it's a good idea to set a nice color to the scene. We can perform this change by applying an **RGBA** (Red, Blue, Green, and Alpha) color to this property, which is a gray color (0.15, 0.15, 0.15,1.0) by default.

Your first game – InsideTheHat

In this game, we will take control of a little rabbit that is trying to escape from the top hat of a magician, where it is trapped. To achieve its objective, our main character will need to run through magic doors until it gets the ace of diamonds that will let the rabbit escape.

In this chapter, we are going to see how to create the main character's sprite and add it to the scene. On the other hand, we will learn how to set a background for the game. In the preceding pages, we have seen a lot of properties and methods that will help us reach our current goal.

Let's start by cleaning off the unnecessary files and content in the project. We are going to generate the screens programmatically so that you can delete the sks file:

1. Right-click on the GameScene.sks file.
2. Choose **Delete**.
3. Ensure that you click on the **Move to Trash** button.

Next, adapt the GameViewController class in order to avoid initializing the scene from the file that we have just removed. Replace the viewDidLoad method from this class with the following block of code:

```
override func viewDidLoad() {
    super.viewDidLoad()

    let scene = GameScene(size: view.bounds.size)
    // Configure the view.
    let skView = self.view as! SKView
    skView.showsFPS = true
    skView.showsNodeCount = true

    /* Sprite Kit applies additional optimizations to improve
rendering performance */
    skView.ignoresSiblingOrder = true
```

```
/* Set the scale mode to scale to fit the window */
scene.scaleMode = .AspectFill

skView.presentScene(scene)
}
```

We have just modified the old line, which looks like this:

```
if let scene = GameScene(fileNamed:"GameScene") {
```

We replaced the preceding line of code with the following code:

```
let scene = GameScene(size: view.bounds.size)
```

This way, we initialized the scene using the init(size:) method of the SKScene class, to which we pass a size value as an input parameter in the form of view.bounds.size. We are using the bounds property of the SKView class, which corresponds to a rectangle that occupies the whole size of the screen.

Now, it's time to clean the GameScene class. Therefore, open it and replace the didMoveToView method with the following piece of code:

```
override func didMoveToView(view: SKView) {
}
```

Replace the touchesBegan method with the following code:

```
override func touchesBegan(touches: Set<UITouch>, withEvent event:
UIEvent?) {
}
```

The project is now ready to be updated with our brand-new code, but you can run it just to ensure that we haven't broken anything.

Our first SKSpriteNode class

The SKSpriteNode class https://developer.apple.com/library/ios/documentation/SpriteKit/Reference/SKSpriteNode_Ref is the one that we are going to use in order to load the sprites that will be a part of our game.

The SKSpriteNode class is a subclass of SKNode, and it's used to represent visual elements called sprites on the screen by using images. As you are going to need an image to create a sprite (an instance of SKSpriteNode class), perform the following steps to add it to the project:

1. Unzip the 7338_01_Resources.zip file in the desired location.

2. In Xcode, right-click on the **InsideTheHat** group on the **Navigator** tab, select **New Group**, and call it **Art**.

3. Right-click on the **Art** group and select **Add Files to InsideTheHat...**.

4. A dialog box will open, where you need to select the rabbit.png image in the 7338_01_Resources folder that you just unzipped.

5. Ensure that **Copy items if needed** is selected and click on **Add**.

Now that the image has been added, we will need a variable to manage the main character. Therefore, on GameScene.swift, add the following line just after class GameScene:SKScene {:

```
private var rabbit: SKSpriteNode!
```

Note that we have declared the variable as a var because its value will change throughout the game's life.

Now that the sprite variable has been declared, modify the didMoveToView method by:

```
override func didMoveToView(view: SKView) {
      self.initializeMainCharacter()
   }

   func initializeMainCharacter() {
      // Creating the rabbit sprite using an image file and adding
it to the scene
   rabbit = SKSpriteNode(imageNamed: "rabbit")

      addChild(rabbit)
   }
```

As soon as the scene is loaded, we call a new method named self.initializeMainCharacter that we created just to keep the code as clean as we can. We will use the self object because we are referencing a method in the current class. If you look at the method, you will see that it initializes the sprite with the init(imageNamed:) method, which takes the image that we have just added to the project to provide the sprite's visual content.

Note that you don't need to specify the extension of the filename, as it will load a `.png`, `.jpg`, `.jpeg`, `.tiff`, `.tif`, `.gif`, `.bmp`, `.BMPf`, `.ico`, `.cur`, or `.xbm` file.

Thanks to this `init` method, the sprite's `size` property (and its `frame`) is automatically set to the dimensions of the image and the color to white `(1.0, 1.0, 1.0)`.

Once the sprite has been initialized, we add it to the scene by using the `addChild` method, which adds a new child to the specified container (`GameScene` in this case), and this is how we add new nodes to the scene.

If you run the game now, you will see something similar to what's shown in the following screenshot:

The sprite has been placed at the bottom left corner of the screen (the (0,0) coordinate), which corresponds to the scene's anchor point. You may be wondering why the rabbit is not fully visible.

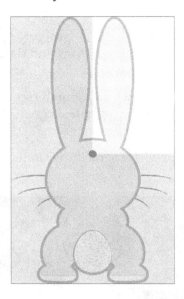

The answer is that the default value of the anchorPoint on an SKSpriteNode is the center of the texture at (0.5, 0.5), while the anchorPoint of the scene is at (0,0). As soon as the sprite is added to the scene, their anchor points get aligned.

For our game, we want the rabbit to be placed at the center of the screen and near at the bottom of the screen. Therefore, add the following lines of code to initializeMainCharacter just before addChild(rabbit):

```
// Positioning the rabbit centered
    rabbit.position = CGPoint(x:(view!.bounds.size.width/2), y:
rabbit.size.height)
```

With the preceding line of code, we created a CGPoint class, which is a commonly used class that is utilized to represent a point in a two-dimensional coordinate system that accepts a CGFloat value for both the *x* and *y* axes. At the bottom-center of the screen, we are setting this point as the position of the rabbit.

Also note how we are getting the center of the screen's width. We get the width property from the size method of the bounds property of the current view (passed as an input argument when the scene is loaded), which is the rectangle that contains all the visual elements. As we want our sprite to be centered on the *x* axis, we just need to divide it by 2, and we have the desired value.

As there are several devices that support iOS and each of them has its own specific resolution and screen sizes, it's very important to always work with relative positions. This way, you don't need to worry about an element's position.

If you look at the code, you will realize that we are setting the sprite's position before adding it to the scene, but you can place it just after the addChild method, and the result won't vary. Now, if you run the game, the rabbit will be placed in the correct position, as shown in the following screenshot:

At this moment, there is nothing that represents that the rabbit is trying to escape from somewhere. Therefore, we need to add context to the game, which is the same as adding a background.

Adding a background

We need to create a road for our rabbit to run on and also for it to find the exit of the top hat. In this case, we will follow almost the same steps than we did to add the rabbit, but with a few differences.

Add the background image in a way that is similar to how we added the rabbit's image:

1. On the **Project Navigator**, select the **Art** group.
2. Right-click and select **Add Files to "InsideTheHat"....**
3. Look for the `background.png` file in the `7338_01_Resources` folder that you unzipped. Select it and click on **Add**.

Then, add the following lines to `GameScene` before the `addChild(rabbit)` line:

```
// Creating and adding the background to the scene
    let background = SKSpriteNode(imageNamed: «background»)
    background.anchorPoint = .zero
    addChild(background)
```

You already know the first line; we are creating a sprite using the background image that we have just added to the project. Then, we set its `anchorPoint` to `.zero`, which is a shortcut for `CGPoint(x:0, y:0)`. The image covers the whole screen, and finally we add the background to the scene.

Run the game. Now, the rabbit should appear standing on a lonely road, as shown in the following screenshot:

You may be wondering why the rabbit sometimes appears and sometimes it doesn't. The reason is that it is behind the background, even though it has been added after the background image.

The reason for this behavior lies in the `skView.ignoresSiblingOrder = true` line in the `GameViewController` class.

The `ignoresSiblingOrder` property indicates whether the relationship between the parent nodes and children affects the order of the nodes in the scene. By default, its value is `false`. This means that SpriteKit will render the children in the same order they appear in the `children` array, one node at a time.

Setting this property to `true` will not take into account the position of the nodes in the tree, but their `zPosition` property groups all the nodes at the same `zPosition` property in a single draw. Therefore, the reason behind setting the `ignoresSiblingOrder` property to `true` is the fact that it will improve the rendering performance.

In the game, the property has been set to `true` and the nodes have no `zPosition` specified (`0.0` by default). This will render all the children on the same time in an arbitrary way. That's why, the rabbit may sometimes be visible and sometime not.

As we want the game to be very efficient, we will keep the `ignoresSiblingOrder` property as is. So, we will need to give the `zPosition` value to some nodes. Open `GameScene` and add the following line just before `addChild(background)`:

```
background.zPosition = -1
```

This way, we set the background behind the default `zPosition` value so that the rest of the nodes that we will add will always be visible. Let's run the game again and check whether the rabbit is now visible. The output is shown in the following screenshot:

Working with screen resolutions

As mentioned previously, iOS games can be executed on devices with different resolutions and screen sizes. This is the reason why it's important to keep in mind the following table, which shows the different families of resolutions and their required file names:

	iPhone 6 Plus	iPhone 6	iPhone 4s, iPhone 5	iPad Retina	iPad
Devices	iPhone 6 Plus, iPhone 6s Plus	iPhone 6, 6s	iPhone 4s iPhone 5, 5C, 5S iPod Touch 5G	iPad Air, Air 2, iPad mini Retina	iPad, iPad 2, iPad mini
Resolution	1242 x 2208	750 x 1334	640 x 960 640 x 1136	1536 x 2048	768 x 1024
File name	file@3x.png	file@2x~iphone.png	file@2x.png	file@2x~ipad.png	file@1x.png

Note that we are showing the devices supported by iOS 9, which is the version that we are using for development purposes.

The above table corresponds to the five resolution families that are available at the time of writing this chapter. In the table, you will see the different devices of each family, their resolutions, and the names that you will need to specify for each of them.

The filenames are composed of a prefix (the filename) and a suffix that can be @3x, @2x~iphone, @2x, @2x~ipad, or @1x (in this case, the suffix can be omitted), depending on the devices that you want the game to be available on.

Providing the needed files will not only result in a better resolution, but also will avoid the programmatic upscaling or downscaling of the image, thus improving the game's performance. Upscaling an image will result in smudgy-looking images but, on the other hand, downscaling images will allow you to reuse a high-resolution image for lower resolution devices. However, this approach is not recommended due to the waste of memory that a non-retina display could lead to.

From now on, when we add a new image to the game, we will need to include the corresponding @2x, @2x~iphone, @2x~ipad and @3x files, if available. Let's add the required images by performing the following steps:

1. In the project navigator, right-click on **Art** and select **Add Files to "InsideTheHat"**....

2. You'll find rabbit@3x.png, rabbit@2x~ipad.png, rabbit@2x.png, background@3x.png, background@2x~ipad.png, and background@2x.png in the 7338_01_Resources folder. Select these four files and click on **Add**.

You can now run the game on other devices and check whether the resolution is maintained in all of them.

Another way of including new image files in a project is by taking advantage of the assets catalog that we mentioned at the beginning of the chapter. If you take a look at this folder, you will see something that is similar to the following screenshot:

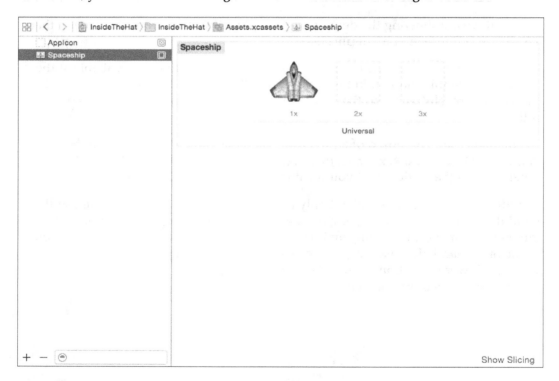

Here, you can create a **New Image Set** by clicking on the **+** button and filling the **1x**, **2x**, and **3x** slots with the corresponding images.

Summary

We started the chapter by looking at a default SpriteKit project, creating a new project, and learning how it is configured and what files it consists of.

You learned what a node is and how to create one with the SKNode class, which is the parent of several important classes that take part in a game. Also, we showed the structure of a scene graph, with a parent SKScene node and several children.

I explained some of the key properties and methods of SKNode and SKScene that will take part in the development of our game. You also had a look at the different steps a game loop requires to render all the contents on the screen.

Then, you learned how to create a scene and add a sprite and a background properly, taking into account their anchor point and their zposition value to ensure that the background lies behind the rest of nodes.

In the last section of this chapter, we explored the characteristics that we need to keep in mind when developing a game for both iPhone and iPad devices, such as screen resolutions and image filenames.

Now that we know how to create a project and load sprites efficiently, let's take a step forward in order to make them interactive and the game playable.

2
What Makes a Game a Game?

In *Chapter 1*, *The First Step toward SpriteKit*, we set the basis of our game by adding a background and the first sprite to our project. In the following pages, I will show you the key elements that take part in every game, such as the movement of sprites in a scene, the detection of touches, and the handling of collisions. You will also learn how to add labels to a scene and play music and sound effects.

The things that you will learn in this chapter are as follows:

- How to detect touch interaction
- How to execute actions on sprites
- How to handle collisions
- Creating and updating labels
- Playing music and sound effects

Handling touch events

Our beloved main character is supposed to run though several doors, but some of them are closed and others are open, so it will need to move laterally to choose the right ones. We will need to handle the players' interaction to help the rabbit properly select a door.

By default, SpriteKit listens to touch events, and we can manage them by implementing some of the methods provided by the UIResponder class, which is the parent class of SKNode.

The following four methods are available if you wish to detect and handle touches:

- The `touchesBegan` method: This method is triggered as soon as the user touches the screen, and it can detect one or more touches. That's why it receives a set of `UITouch` instances. We can use this method to select the place where we want the rabbit to be moved in the game.

- The `touchesMoved` method: This method will be triggered when one or more fingers that are touching the screen begin to move. We can take advantage of this method to update a node's position while it is being dragged.

- The `touchesEnded` method: This method will be triggered as soon as one or more fingers that are touching the screen are released and they are no longer touching the screen. This method can be useful when you want to recognize when a user wants to stop dragging a node.

- The `touchesCancelled` method: We can implement this method in order to execute actions when a touch event is finished due to some system event, such as a phone call or a memory warning.

From these methods, we will take advantage of the `touchesBegan` method, which is inheriting from `SKScene` class, which is inheriting from the `UIResponder` class. For this purpose, open `GameScene.swift` and implement `touchesBegan` using the following lines:

```
if let touch = touches.first {
    // Moving the rabbit to the touched position
    let location = touch.locationInNode(self)
    self.moveRabbitToNextLocation(location)
}
```

As a device detects all the touches on the screen, the `touches` object will contain a set of `UITouch` instances. From here, you can get the first instances of them by executing the `first` method.

Once we have one single touch event, we just need to know where it is placed. This task is very easy to perform as we just need to call the `locationInNode` method and pass the node where the touch event has taken place (the scene), and we will get the `CGPoint` function corresponding to it.

Once we have the location of the touch, we just need to pass it to the `moveRabbitToNextLocation` method, where all the magic is going to happen. To know what this method does, add the following code after the `touchesBegan` method:

```
func moveRabbitToNextLocation(touchLocation: CGPoint) {
    // The constant rabbit's speed
```

```
let rabbitSpeed: CGFloat = 360.0

var moveAction:SKAction!
var duration: CGFloat = 0.0
var nextPosition: CGPoint

if touchLocation.x <= view!.bounds.size.width/3 {
    // Setting the next position
    nextPosition = CGPoint(x: view!.bounds.size.width/6 + 25 *
rabbit.frame.width/40, y: rabbit.position.y)
    // We want the rabbit to move on a constant speed
    duration = self.distanceBetween(point: rabbit.position,
andPoint: nextPosition) / rabbitSpeed
    // Move the rabbit to the touched position
    moveAction = SKAction.moveToX(nextPosition.x, duration:
Double(duration))
} else if touchLocation.x > view!.bounds.size.width/3 &&
touchLocation.x <= 2 * view!.bounds.size.width/3 {
    // Setting the next position
    nextPosition = CGPoint(x: view!.bounds.size.width/2, y:
rabbit.position.y)
    // We want the rabbit to move on a constant speed
    duration = self.distanceBetween(point: rabbit.position,
andPoint: nextPosition) / rabbitSpeed
    // Move the rabbit to the touched position
    moveAction = SKAction.moveToX(nextPosition.x, duration:
Double(duration))
} else {
    // Setting the next position
    nextPosition = CGPoint(x: 5*view!.bounds.size.width/6 - 25 *
rabbit.frame.width/40, y: rabbit.position.y)
    // We want the rabbit to move on a constant speed
    duration = self.distanceBetween(point: rabbit.position,
andPoint: nextPosition) / rabbitSpeed
    // Move the rabbit to the touched position
    moveAction = SKAction.moveToX(nextPosition.x, duration:
Double(duration))
}
// Executing the action
rabbit.runAction(moveAction)
}
```

Okay, I know that it's a big piece of code, but don't worry. It's very easy to understand. We want to move the little rabbit laterally with a constant speed (360.0). That's why we declared the `rabbitSpeed`, `moveAction`, `duration`, and `nextPosition` variables.

The rabbit will need to choose between the three doors that are placed at the center of each third of the screen's width. That's why, after declaring the variables, we need to check whether the touch event has taken place on any third of the screen's width.

For example, let's pay attention to the first condition:

```
if touchLocation.x <= view!.bounds.size.width/3{
```

With this line, we are checking whether the *x* coordinate of the touch location is lower than the view's width divided by 3 (the third of the screen on the left). If this condition is fulfilled, we initialize the `nextPosition` variable with the coordinates of the desired location, which corresponds to the screen position at the middle of each of the three doors that the rabbit will need to avoid.

So, once we know the next position, we just need to focus on the movement itself. SpriteKit provides a large number of methods to perform all the actions that we will need in a game. At this moment, we will just focus on movement actions and specifically on `moveToX`, which will move a sprite to a desired position (taking into account only the *x* coordinate) in a specified duration and can be concurrently called, resulting in a movement that will be the sum of the different movements. There are similar actions, such as `moveToY`, `moveToX` (a specific point), and `moveBy`, that generate a movement to the next position using relative coordinates. However, we want to move to an absolute position to ensure that we pass through the doors properly.

As we want the rabbit to always move at the same speed (360.0), we will need to update the duration of the action using basic physics. Do you remember the formula to calculate speed?

```
time = distance/speed
```

We already know the speed, but we need to calculate the distance between the main character and its `nextPosition` value. Then we will be able to get the time (`duration`) that this movement will last.

For the purpose of calculating the distance between the rabbit and its desired position, I've implemented a very useful method named distanceBetween, which will retrieve the value that we are looking for. Add the following method to GameScene:

```
func distanceBetween(point p1:CGPoint, andPoint p2:CGPoint) -> CGFloat
{
    return sqrt(pow((p2.x - p1.x), 2) + pow((p2.y - p1.y), 2))
}
```

This method is basic mathematics; it returns the distance between the points named p1 and p2. Once we have the distance and the speed values, we can calculate the duration value and create the movement action by specifying the position and the time we want the action to last.

The last line in the moveRabbitToNextLocation method is rabbit. runAction(moveAction). This line will trigger the action, and without it, there won't be any movement at all, as it sends the runAction message with the action that we just created for the node that we want to move.

Okay, that's enough code for now. Run the project and see how the rabbit happily moves left and right:

However, if you touch on the screen several times, you will notice that the `movement` action behaves in a strange way. Don't worry, it's due to the `moveToX` nature itself. When I introduced this action, I specified that it can be concurrently called, resulting in a movement that will be the sum of the individual movements. But in our case, it's making the rabbit look a bit crazy. To take control of the actions, we need to be aware of some methods that can be used to stop them whenever we need to.

Handling actions

In SpriteKit, we can trigger and stop actions whenever we want. In this way, we can control what is happening at every moment thanks to a collection of methods provided by `SKNode`, which are as follows:

- `hasActions()`: This method returns a Boolean value that indicates whether a node is running an action. We can take advantage of this method to check whether we can run an action, as it may cause some wrong behavior if it takes place at the same time as that of existing actions.

- `runAction(_:)`: As previously discussed, this method runs the `SKAction` object as an input parameter.

- `runAction(_:, completion:)`: This method is similar to the previous one; the only difference is that with this method, we can specify a block of code that we want to execute as soon as an action finishes. For example, this will be very useful if we want to reset an enemy's position when its movement is completed.

- `runAction(_:, withKey:)`: With this method, we can specify a character chain to indicate an action. In this way, we will be able to have direct control over the action.

- `actionForKey(_:)`: This method will allow us to get a specified key in order to retrieve an action if it exists. If there is no matching key, it will return a nil value.

- `removeAllActions()`: This method will stop all the running actions in a node. However, when an action is removed, it may make a final change to the scene as it corresponds to the changes prior to the removal.

- `removeActionForKey(_:)`: If we have stored the key value of an action that was run before, we can use it to stop the action directly and leave the rest of the actions running.

All of these methods can be useful during a game's development. In fact, we will make use of several of these methods in the following sections. In our case, we just want to stop all actions so that they don't concatenate and result in strange behavior.

We just need to make one change in the code. In `touchesBegan`, add the following lines just after `if let touch = touches.first {`:

```
// Controlling actions
if rabbit.hasActions() {
    rabbit.removeAllActions()
}
```

If you run the game now, you will realize that the rabbit's movement doesn't exhibit any weird behavior even when you touch the screen several times.

Building a wall

When the game starts, the rabbit will start running, trying to find the exit of the top hat. In its course, it will need to avoid closed doors. For this purpose, we need to create a wall. So let's start by adding the needed images:

1. Unzip the `7338_02_Resources.zip` and go back to **Xcode**.

2. Right-click on **Art** and select **Add Files to InsideTheHat…**.

3. You'll find `wall.png`, `wall@2x.png`, `wall@2x~ipad.png`, `wall@2x~iphone.png`, and `wall@3x.png` in the `7338_02_Resources` folder that you just unzipped. Select these five files and click on **Add**.

Now that we have the resources, let's call the method that will create the wall. Add the following code at the end of the `didMoveToView` method of `GameScene`:

```
self.initializeWall()
```

Before implementing the method, we will need to declare a variable for the wall in a way that is similar to how we declared a variable for the rabbit. Add the following line just after the declaration of the `rabbit` variable:

```
private var wall: SKSpriteNode!
```

Now, implement the `initializeWall` method with the following block of code:

```
func initializeWall() {
    // Creating the wall sprite using an image file
    wall = SKSpriteNode(imageNamed: "wall")
    // Positioning the wall centered
    wall.position = CGPoint(x:(view!.bounds.size.width/2), y: view!.
bounds.size.height/2)
    // Specifying zPosition
    wall.zPosition = 2
    // Adding the wall to the scene
    addChild(wall)
}
```

This method is pretty similar to the one that we used to create the rabbit. We initialized the `wall` variable using the image that we just provided. Then, we set its position just at the center of the screen. Finally, we added the new node to the scene. We have chosen the center of the screen just to see how the wall looks, but it will change in the following section.

We also specified the `zPosition` value of the wall in order to achieve the result that we want after adding all the objects that are needed in the scene.

Time to run the game and check out how it looks so far:

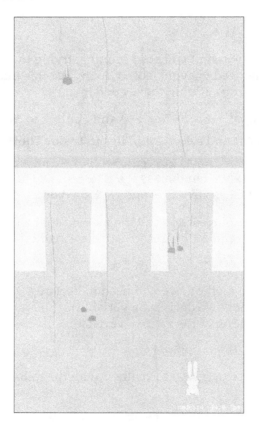

Running through the doors

In this section, we are going to manage the wall's behavior. As we are simulating that the little rabbit is running, it will need to avoid the doors and the wall that will appear at the top of the screen. To simulate the rabbit's run, we will move the walls from the top to the bottom of the screen, and we already have the needed knowledge to perform this task.

First of all, we will need to place the original wall's position outside the screen. You need to replace the following line in `initializeWall`:

```
wall.position = CGPoint(x: (view!.bounds.size.width/2), y: view!.
bounds.size.height/2)
```

The preceding line should be replaced by the following code:

```
wall.position = CGPoint(x: (view!.bounds.size.width/2), y: view!.
bounds.size.height + wall.frame.size.height/2)
```

In this way, we have set the wall in the position that's shown in the following screenshot:

Now that the wall is in its initial position, it's time to apply some movement to it. So, let's call a new method by adding the following lines of code at the end of the didMoveToView method of GameScene:

```
self.initializeWallMovement()
```

Implement this using the following block of code:

```
func initializeWallMovement() {
    // The constant wall's speed
    let wallSpeed: CGFloat = 250.0
    // Setting the wall's final position
    let nextWallPosition = CGPoint(x: wall.position.x, y: -wall.frame.
size.height/2)
    // We want the wall to move on a constant speed
    let duration = self.distanceBetween(point: wall.position,
andPoint: nextWallPosition) / wallSpeed
    // Move the wall to the next position
    let moveWallAction = SKAction.moveToY(nextWallPosition.y,
duration: Double(duration))

    // Reset the wall's position
    let resetPositionAction = SKAction.runBlock {
    self.wall.position = CGPoint(x:(self.view!.bounds.size.width/2),
y: self.view!.bounds.size.height + self.wall.frame.size.height/2)
    }

    // Executing the actions
    wall.runAction(SKAction.sequence([moveWallAction,
resetPositionAction]))
}
```

The preceding code is very similar to the one that we used to move the rabbit. We first declare a constant variable for the wall's speed, and we specify the final position that we want the wall to reach. Note that this final position is centered outside the view, but on the bottom of the screen this time.

As we want the wall to move at a constant speed, we calculate the duration with the same strategy that we used for the rabbit. Then, we create a moveToY action with these values, as we just want the object to be scrolled vertically.

Once the movement action is done, we want the wall to recover its initial position. That's why, we are going to take advantage of a special type of SKAction instances named sequence. A sequence is an action that allows us to synchronously execute an array of actions so that the first instance in an array will run first and, as soon as it ends, it will trigger the second action in the array, and so on.

Now that we know what a sequence is, we need a way to reset the wall's position. That's why, we will declare `resetPositionAction`, a `runBlock` action that allows us to execute all the code that we want whenever we need to. If you look at the block of code, you will see that we just specified the original wall's position.

 One important thing that you need to keep in mind when coding blocks is the scope of the variables. As we want to use a class variable, we need to specify `self.wall` or `self.view`.

Finally, we will execute a sequence with both the required actions in order to achieve the desired behavior. Run the game at this point, and you will see how the node disappears at the bottom of the screen. If you want, you can reset the position to a visible one so that you can check whether the sequence is running properly:

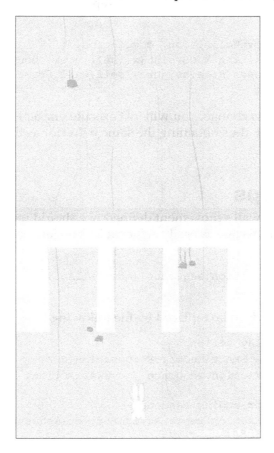

1-star challenge: an easier way to reset position

I chose the solution of running two actions in order to recover the initial position because I wanted to introduce you to sequences, but there is an easier and fancier way of achieving the same result. With the knowledge that you have so far, try to get the same results that you got when using a sequence.

Solution

The key to this challenge is to use the `runAction(_:, completion:)` method so that we can execute the same block of code as that of `resetPositionAction`. Go to the `initializeWallMovement` method and replace `moveWallAction` with the following code:

```
wall.runAction(moveWallAction, completion: {
    self.wall.position = CGPoint(x:(self.view!.bounds.size.width/2),
y: self.view!.bounds.size.height + self.wall.frame.size.height/2)
})
```

There you are. With this change, you will just execute one action with a completion block associated with it, thus obtaining the same behavior as the one that you got before.

Creating loops

Now that we have the wall's movement defined, we should repeat it when the game is running, and this task is easily achievable. You just need to replace the following line:

```
wall.runAction(SKAction.sequence([moveWallAction,
resetPositionAction]))
```

The preceding line needs to be replaced by the following lines of code:

```
// Creating a delay action
let delayAction = SKAction.waitForDuration(2.0)
let sequence = SKAction.sequence([moveWallAction, resetPositionAction,
delayAction])
// Running the non-ending sequence
wall.runAction(SKAction.repeatActionForever(sequence))
```

In the preceding block of code, we first declared a delay action, which is typically used to introduce a waiting period of time before another action happens. We have specified the delayAction value as 2.0 because this is the time the wall will wait until its movement.

Then, we modified the sequence to include this new action at the end of the process. Finally, we run the repeatActionForever method, which will create an unending loop of the wall's movement. You can check this behavior by running the game. Now that we have a way to create loops, let's add some doors to the scene so that the game makes more sense.

Installing doors into the wall

In this section, we are going to follow the same solution that we used for the walls but with a small change. Let's start by declaring a new variable for each door. Add the following lines after private var wall: SKSpriteNode!:

```
private var leftDoor: SKSpriteNode!
private var centerDoor: SKSpriteNode!
private var rightDoor: SKSpriteNode!
```

As we will need some images for these new nodes, we first have to add them to the project. Perform the following steps for this purpose:

1. Right-click on **Art** and select **Add Files to InsideTheHat…**.
2. You'll find wrong_door.png, correct_door.png, wrong_door@2x. png, correct_door@2x.png, wrong_door@2x~ipad.png, correct_ door@2x~ipad.png, wrong_door@2x~iphone.png, correct_ door@2x~iphone.png, wrong_door@3x.png, and correct_door@3x.png in the 7338_02_Resources folder that you just unzipped. Select these 10 files and click on **Add**.

Now, add the following line at the end of the didMoveToView function:

```
self.initializeDoors()
```

And implement it with this block of code:

```
func initializeDoors() {
    // Initializing left door
    self.setDoorAttributes("left")
    // Positioning left door
    leftDoor.position = CGPoint(x:(view!.bounds.size.width/2) - (25
* leftDoor.frame.size.width / 20), y: self.view!.bounds.size.height +
leftDoor.frame.size.height/2)
```

```
    // Specifying zPosition
    leftDoor.zPosition = 0
    // Adding the door to the scene
    addChild(leftDoor)

    // Initializing center door
    self.setDoorAttributes("center")
    // Positioning center door
    centerDoor.position = CGPoint(x:(view!.bounds.size.width/2), y:
self.view!.bounds.size.height + centerDoor.frame.size.height/2)
    // Specifying zPosition
    centerDoor.zPosition = 0
    // Adding the door to the scene
    addChild(centerDoor)

    // Initializing right door
    self.setDoorAttributes("right")
    // Positioning right door
    rightDoor.position = CGPoint(x:(view!.bounds.size.width/2) + (25
* rightDoor.frame.size.width / 20), y: self.view!.bounds.size.height +
rightDoor.frame.size.height/2)
    // Specifying zPosition
    rightDoor.zPosition = 0
    // Adding the door to the scene
    addChild(rightDoor)
}
```

In this method, we initialized the three doors in the same way. We first executed the `setDoorAttributes` function, which created the node and set other attributes. Then, we specified the door's initial position (out of the view and at the top of the screen), which will be placed at the corresponding door's opening. Finally, we specified its `zPosition` property and we added the door to the scene.

As you can see, we called the `setDoorAttributes` function using the `left`, `center`, and `right` input parameters, depending on the door's position. To understand this, we implement `setDoorAttributes` function by adding the following lines of code to `GameScene`:

```
func setDoorAttributes(position: String) {
    switch position {
        case "wrong_left_door", "correct_left_door", "left":
        // Setting the door sprite randomly
        if (arc4random_uniform(2) == 0) {
```

```
                // Initialize the door if null
                if (leftDoor == nil) {
                    leftDoor = SKSpriteNode(imageNamed: "wrong_door")
                }
                // Update texture and name attributes
                leftDoor.texture = SKTexture(imageNamed: "wrong_door")
                leftDoor.name = "wrong_left_door"
                } else {
                    // Initialize the door if null
                    if (leftDoor == nil) {
                        leftDoor = SKSpriteNode(imageNamed: "correct_
door")
                    }
                    // Update texture and name attributes
                    leftDoor.texture = SKTexture(imageNamed: "correct_
door")
                    leftDoor.name = "correct_left_door"
                }

        default: break
    }
}
```

This method expects a `String` value that will represent the position of the door that we want to modify. This value will be used in a `switch` statement in order to match with any of the different types of doors.

The different values that we expect for the left door are `left`, which will correspond to the door that was just created; `wrong_left_door`, which corresponds to a left door whose texture name is `wrong_door`; and `correct_left_door`, which will correspond to a left door whose texture name is `correct_door`. I know that these last values are a little weird, but if you keep reading, you will fully understand why I chose this approach.

The first aspect of every door case is about randomly deciding whether we are creating a wrong door or a correct one. For this purpose, we will use the `arc4random_uniform(n)` method, which will return a uniformly distributed random value between `0` and `n-1`.

If this random value is equal to `0`, we first initialize the `leftDoor` sprite if it hasn't been initialized yet. Then, we check whether it has been initialized because we want to reuse this method. Also, we will avoid creating a new node each time and maintain the performance of the game this way.

Next, we set the correct `texture` value and specify a `name` value in order to easily identify the node.

This block is repeated for the correct door when the random value is 1. Therefore, we don't need to get into the details. Just check whether the texture and name are properly set.

The bottom piece of code just represents the `default` case of the `switch` statement, which will do nothing in this case.

The previous code just initializes the `leftDoor` variable. Add the following block of code just before `default: break` for the door at the center of the screen:

```
case "wrong_center_door", "correct_center_door", "center":
    // Setting the door sprite randomly
    if (arc4random_uniform(2) == 0) {
        // Initialize the door if null
        if (centerDoor == nil) {
            centerDoor = SKSpriteNode(imageNamed: "wrong_door")
        }
        // Update texture and name attributes
        centerDoor.texture = SKTexture(imageNamed: "wrong_door")
        centerDoor.name = "wrong_center_door"
    }else {
        // Initialize the door if null
        if (centerDoor == nil) {
            centerDoor = SKSpriteNode(imageNamed: "correct_door")
        }
        // Update texture and name attributes
        centerDoor.texture = SKTexture(imageNamed: "correct_door")
        centerDoor.name = "correct_center_door"
    }
```

This code will create the center door properly, depending on the random value, if the sprite node has been created previously. Copy the following lines of code to create the right door:

```
case "wrong_right_door", "correct_right_door", "right":
    // Setting the door sprite randomly
    if (arc4random_uniform(2) == 0) {
        // Initialize the door if null
        if (rightDoor == nil) {
            rightDoor = SKSpriteNode(imageNamed: "wrong_door")
        }
        // Update texture and name attributes
        rightDoor.texture = SKTexture(imageNamed: "wrong_door")
```

```
        rightDoor.name = "wrong_right_door"
    } else {
        // Initialize the door if null
        if (rightDoor == nil) {
            rightDoor = SKSpriteNode(imageNamed: "correct_door")
        }
        // Update texture and name attributes
        rightDoor.texture = SKTexture(imageNamed: "correct_door")
        rightDoor.name = "correct_right_door"
}
```

Now that the doors have been initialized, it's time to define its movement. Add the following lines of code at the end of `didMoveToView`:

```
self.initializeDoorsMovement()
```

Implement this using the following lines:

```
func initializeDoorsMovement() {
    // The constant door's speed
    let doorSpeed: CGFloat = 250.0

    var leftDoorAction: SKAction!
    var centerDoorAction: SKAction!
    var rightDoorAction: SKAction!

    self.enumerateChildNodesWithName("*_door") {
        node, stop in
    }
}
```

In this piece of code, we declared a float variable for the doors' speed, which is the same value as that of the wall's speed. Furthermore, we declared three `SKAction` variables, one for each door.

In the last block of code, we executed the `enumerateChildNodesWithName` method of the scene by passing the `*_door` regular expression, which means that which will match the doors' names: `wrong_left_door`, `correct_left_door`, `wrong_center_door`, `correct_center_door`, `wrong_right_door`, and `correct_right_door`. In this call, `node` makes a reference to each child on the enumeration, and `stop` is a variable that we can set to `true` whenever we want the enumeration to end.

Let's add the following lines of code to the previous code:

```
// Setting the door's final position
let nextDoorPosition = CGPoint(x: node.position.x, y: -(self.wall.
frame.size.height - node.frame.size.height / 2))
// We want the door to move on a constant speed
let duration = self.distanceBetween(point: node.position, andPoint:
nextDoorPosition) / doorSpeed
// Move the door to the next position
let moveDoorAction = SKAction.moveToY(nextDoorPosition.y, duration:
Double(duration))
```

These lines are pretty similar to the ones that we used to move the wall. We first specified the position that we want each door to reach. Then, we calculated the duration for which this movement will last, which will be used to declare a `moveToY` action.

Note that we are setting the final position of the door. The position of the door will have final position, that moves with the wall as a unique block.

Now, add the following lines after the preceding code:

```
// Reset the door's position
let resetPositionAction = SKAction.runBlock {
    // Reset door's attributes
    self.setDoorAttributes(node.name!)
    node.position = CGPoint(x:node.position.x, y: self.view!.bounds.
size.height + node.frame.size.height/2)
}
```

We declared a `runBlock` action in order to set its texture and name again once its movement finishes. In this way, the doors' type will change after each wave.

The `resetPositionAction` action will also reset the door's initial position. Therefore, the next time the node starts moving, it will be from the correct position.

Now, let's complete the `enumerateChildNodesWithName` block by adding the following lines of code just after the `resetPositionAction` declaration:

```
// Preparing the actions
let delayAction = SKAction.waitForDuration(2.0)
let sequence = SKAction.sequence([moveDoorAction, resetPositionAction,
delayAction])

// Set the sequence into the correct door
switch node.name! {
    case "wrong_left_door", "correct_left_door":
        leftDoorAction = SKAction.repeatActionForever(sequence)
    case "wrong_center_door", "correct_center_door":
        centerDoorAction = SKAction.repeatActionForever(sequence)
    case "wrong_right_door", "correct_right_door":
        rightDoorAction = SKAction.repeatActionForever(sequence)
    default: break
}
```

In this block, we created an `action` to use it as a delay. Then, we declared a `sequence` event with the three actions that we have prepared. Next, we used a `switch` statement in order to initialize each of the doors' actions, depending on the name of the node, as a `repeatActionForever`.

Finally, we just need to execute these actions. Add the following lines at the end of `initializeDoorsMovement` just after `enumerateChildNodesWithName`:

```
// Running door's actions
leftDoor.runAction(leftDoorAction)
centerDoor.runAction(centerDoorAction)
rightDoor.runAction(rightDoorAction)
```

The preceding code just runs the three doors' actions. It's time to check out what we have just done. Run the project and look at how the wall and the doors move:

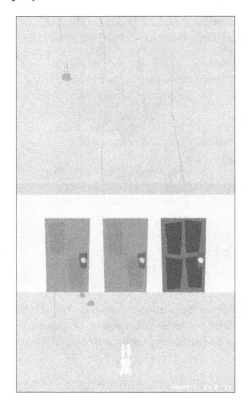

We could have achieved the same results in other ways, but I decided to use the `enumerateChildNodesWithName` way to show you how this method works and in order to avoid duplicating code three times.

Before moving on to the explanation, let's adjust the rabbit's `zPosition` value in order to be above the doors but below the wall. Just add the following line of code to the `initializeMainCharacter` method before initializing the background node:

```
// Specifying zPosition
rabbit.zPosition = 1
```

Collision management

In the previous section of this chapter, we learned the most important techniques to perform actions on nodes, namely movements. Now that everything is moving, we need a way to detect when the main character tries to cross a closed door (a wrong door) or an open one (a correct door).

Detecting and handling collisions is one of the main techniques in game development, as a vast percentage of games is founded upon enemies trying to hit our character in many different ways or the player trying to *kill* the enemies by shooting them, jumping at them, and so on. But, what is a collision?

Understanding collisions

In game development, a collision is an intersection between two or more elements in a scene. There are different ways to detect them, from the most basic's such as checking whether the area of the frame of each node intersects other nodes' frames, to the advanced ones such as making use of the physics engines that most of the games' engines (including SpriteKit) provide.

Our game's logic is pretty simple. The rabbit just has to avoid colliding with some doors. We will go through the basic collision detection, which will consist of detecting whether the rabbit's frame hits a wrong door's frame.

Handling collisions

For this purpose, we will need to check collisions of each frame, and the best way to achieve this is by making use of the `update` method provided by `GameScene`.

Let's start by creating a Boolean variable that will be used to check whether a collision has already happened. Add the following line in the variable declaration section of `GameScene`:

```
private var isCollisionDetected: Bool = false
```

This variable will help us avoid unnecessary checks and actions since in each game's frame, when the rabbit collides with a door (which will happen several times when the rabbit passes through it), the collision detection will be raised. We have taken advantage of its declaration to initialize it to `false`, as there hasn't been any collision so far.

Now, in the auxiliary Boolean variable, add the following block of code to the `update` method:

```
// Detect collisions
if !self.isCollisionDetected {
    self.detectCollisions()
}
```

If there haven't been any colliding nodes, we call the `detectCollisions` method. Implement it using the following block of code:

```
func detectCollisions() {
    self.enumerateChildNodesWithName("*_door") {
        node, stop in

        // Check if the frames intersect
        if node.frame.intersects(self.rabbit.frame) {
            if node.name?.containsString("wrong") == true {
                // Collision detected
                self.isCollisionDetected = true

                // Make the rabbit blink
                let blinkAction = SKAction.sequence([
                    SKAction.colorizeWithColor(UIColor.redColor(),
colorBlendFactor: 0.5, duration: 0.1),
                    SKAction.fadeAlphaTo(0.0, duration: 0.2),
                    SKAction.fadeAlphaTo(1.0, duration: 0.2),
                    SKAction.colorizeWithColor(UIColor.whiteColor(),
colorBlendFactor: 1.0, duration: 0.1),
                    ])
                self.rabbit.runAction(SKAction.
repeatAction(blinkAction, count: 3))
            }
            // Make door invisible
            node.hidden = true
        }
    }
}
```

In this method, we took advantage of the already known `enumerateChildNodesWithName` method to iterate through all the doors in the scene. Then, for each door, we execute the `intersects` method, which is a utility provided by `CGRect` to check whether two frames intersect. The rabbit's frame is passed as an input parameter.

If this check returns `true`, it means that the collision has happened. However, we need to ensure that the collided door is a wrong door. That's why we check whether the node's name contains the word `wrong`.

If both conditions happen, we update the Boolean flag to avoid unnecessary checks and improve the game's performance.

To represent that the rabbit has collided with one door, we are going to make it blink and change its color to red in less than a second. That's why, we declare a new action as a sequence of four actions.

The first action of this sequence is `colorizeWithColor`, which allows us to change the color of the rabbit to red. This color change will increase gradually in the specified `duration` value and with the strength set as `colorBlendFactor` (the higher this factor, the more opaque the color).

The second action is a `fadeAlphaTo` function, which will change the alpha value of the node to `0.0` and make it invisible.

The last two actions in the sequence will recover the alpha and the white color of the node respectively.

Finally, we run the sequences into a `repeatAction` function with a `count` value of 3, which means that we will make the rabbit blink three times when it collides with a wrong door.

The last line of code in the method will hide the node to simulate that the door was open or crashed when the rabbit crossed it.

Now that we have included the code that's necessary to check and react to collisions, we just need to recover the flag's value when we know that no other collision will happen and make the node visible again, which will be done as soon as the doors reach their final positions.

For this purpose, we need to add the following lines at the end of the `resetPositionAction` block of `initializeDoorsMovement`:

```
// Make door visible
node.hidden = false
// Revert flag's value
if self.isCollisionDetected {
    self.isCollisionDetected = false
}
```

In this way, when we recover the door's position, we recover its visibility at the same time and update the flag's value to begin detecting collisions again.

Okay, enough of coding for now. Run the game and check out what happens when the rabbit tries to cross the wrong doors:

1-star challenge: check collisions accurately

We learned how to detect collisions thanks to the `intersects` method provided by `CGRect`, but in this way, the collision will be triggered as soon as the rabbit's ears touch the doors. Let's add another condition to the `if` statement in `detectCollisions` in order to take into account the rabbit's and door's frame position. Thus, the collision will only happen when the door reaches half the rabbit's frame. As shown in the following screenshot:

Solution

This challenge is very easy and I hope you were able to solve it. To perform this check, you just need to add the following condition to the `if` statement:

```
&& (node.position.y - node.frame.height/2) <= self.rabbit.position.y
```

Keep this line in the code as we are going to use this condition in order to make the collisions more realistic.

Creating labels

In almost every game, there are different elements (scores or text labels) to provide visual information to the player and give them an incentive to keep playing in order to beat its score record. In this section, we are going to learn how to add these informative elements to a scene.

In SpriteKit, we have a class named `SKLabelNode` that inherits from `SKNode` and provides all the methods and attributes to load fonts and manage every label that we want to show on the screen. We are going to use this class to add a score label at the top-right side of the screen and update it, as the rabbit avoids wrong doors.

Let's start by creating our first label. Then, we will learn how to update it programmatically. For this purpose, we are going to need a new variable. So, add the following line to GameScene just after the declaration of isCollisionDetected:

```
private var labelScore: SKLabelNode!
```

Next, we need to call a method to initialize it. So, add the following line at the end of didMoveToView:

```
self.initializeLabels()
```

Implement this by adding the following block of code:

```
func initializeLabels() {
    // Initialize the label with a font name
    labelScore = SKLabelNode(fontNamed:"MarkerFelt-Thin")
    // Set color, size and position
    labelScore.fontColor = UIColor.blackColor()
    labelScore.fontSize = 20
    labelScore.position = CGPoint(x:(3 * labelScore.fontSize),
y:(view!.bounds.size.height - 2 * labelScore.fontSize))
    // Specifying zPosition
    labelScore.zPosition = 3

    // Set text
    labelScore.text = "Score: 0"

    // Add the label to the scene
    addChild(labelScore)
}
```

The first thing that we did in this method was initialize the node using MarkerFelt-Thin as its font name. I chose this font as it will be easily visible on the screen, but you can try whatever you want from the ones available for iOS. For more information, visit https://support.apple.com/en-us/HT202771.

Once we have created a label, we can modify some of its attributes. For example, in the previous method, we specified that we want the label's node to be black and the font size is set to 20, which is big enough for the screen. If you paid attention, we modified the fontColor property in spite of color, as the last property is combined with colorBlendFactor to modify the node's tint and not the font color.

Next, we set the label's position on the top-left side of the screen, as we want to leave the major part of the view free for the game. Note how we are using relative values for both the x and y coordinates. In this way, the label's position will be equivalent on different devices.

Finally, we specified the `zPosition` value for the label and we set an initial text for the label, which would be the initial score value, and we added it to the scene.

Come on, run the project and look at the text on the screen:

Now that we know how to create labels, let's update the score label, which will happen when the rabbit crosses a correct door.

For this purpose, we are going to follow an approach which involves using a flag that will be updated at the end of each wave, when the group of doors reach their final position at the bottom of the screen. In this way, we will know when a wave ends, which is when we need to check whether a collision happened. In case there were no collisions, the score will be increased by 10 points.

Let's start by initializing the variables that we will need to achieve our goal. Add the following lines to `GameScene`:

```
private var resetWave: Bool = false
private var score: Int = 0
```

As you can see, we are going to use a Boolean flag to know when a wave ends (initialized to `false`) and, on the other hand, we will need an integer variable to store the score reached so far by the player.

The first thing that we need to modify is the line where we set the text into the label, as we don't want hardcoded pieces of code. So, you need to replace the following line in `initializeLabels`:

```
labelScore.text = "Score: 0"
```

Replace the preceding line with the following code:

```
labelScore.text = "Score: \(score)"
```

As you can see, we have set the `\(score)` function in a string. This Swift utility will print the value of the score variable into the character's chain.

Next, we need to scrutinize every frame to check whether the wave has ended. We will need to perform this check in the `update` method by adding the following block of code:

```
// If a new wave has to start
if resetWave {
    self.initializeWave()
}
```

This means that when a wave has ended, we will trigger the following method:

```
func initializeWave() {
    if self.isCollisionDetected {
        // Revert flag's value
        self.isCollisionDetected = false
    } else {
        // Update score if collision avoided
        self.score += 10
        self.labelScore.text = "Score: \(self.score)"
    }
    //Update flag
    self.resetWave = false
}
```

In this method, we reset the flag that helps us identify collisions (if a collision occurred), as we need to start looking for collisions again. If there hasn't been any collision, we update the score by increasing its value by 10 points, and we also update the label as we did previously. Finally, we revert the `resetWave` flag to false to restart the wave.

However, there is one thing left. We need a place to update the wave's flag, and this place is at the end of each door's movement. In other words, it's present at the end of `resetPositionAction` in `initializeDoorsMovement`. You just need to replace the following code:

```
// Revert flag's value
if self.isCollisionDetected {
    self.isCollisionDetected = false
}
```

Replace the preceding code with the following lines:

```
// The doors wave will restart
self.resetWave = true
```

In this way, we identify when a wave has ended by updating the flag, and we remove the part related to `isCollisionDetected`, as we have included it in `initializeWave`.

If you now run the game, you will see that the game works perfectly:

Aligning labels

Now that we have a label on the screen, we should take into account whether its size will change along the course of the gameplay. For example, the score label will change for sure, as the player is expected to choose the correct doors, therefore, the label width will increase fast.

In our case, the label is placed at the top-left side of the screen. So, we will not experience this behavior, but, what if we have a label on the right-hand side that will increase in size?

Let's change some things in the label. We'll start by moving it to the right-hand side. You need to replace the following line in `initializeLabels`:

```
labelScore.position = CGPoint(x:(3 * labelScore.fontSize), y:(view!.
bounds.size.height - 2 * labelScore.fontSize))
```

Replace the preceding code with the following one:

```
labelScore.position = CGPoint(x:(view!.bounds.size.width - 2 *
labelScore.fontSize), y:(view!.bounds.size.height - 2 * labelScore.
fontSize))
```

In this way, we have placed the score label on the right-hand side of the screen. If you run the game now and start avoiding the wrong doors, you will see how the label's width grows as the score increases. The problem is that a part of the label lies out of view, and this behavior is a little weird. So, let's use some magic to solve it.

The `SKLabelNode` class provides two attributes that allow us to align our labels: `verticalAlignmentMode` and `horizontalAlignmentMode`.

The first one indicates the vertical position of the text relative to the node's position and can take one of the following values:

- `SKLabelVerticalAlignmentMode.Baseline`: This is the default value and, thanks to it, the text's baseline will lie at the origin of the label node.

- `SKLabelVerticalAlignmentMode.Center`: This value will vertically center the text on the label's origin.

- `SKLabelVerticalAlignmentMode.Top`: This value will place the text's top on the origin of the label node.

- `SKLabelVerticalAlignmentMode.Bottom`: This value will place the text's bottom on the origin of the label node.

On the other hand, we can align labels horizontally thanks to horizontalAlignmentMode and the following different values that it can take:

- SKLabelHorizontalAlignmentMode.Center: This is the default value, and the text can be centered horizontally on the label's origin with this value.
- SKLabelHorizontalAlignmentMode.Left: The text's left side will be on the origin of the label node if you use this value.
- SKLabelHorizontalAlignmentMode.Right: The text's right side will be on the origin of the label node if you use this value.

Now that we are aware of these properties, let's apply them, specifically the horizontal alignment, to our game. Go back to the initializeLabels method and add the following line just before labelScore.text = "Score: \(score)":

```
labelScore.horizontalAlignmentMode = SKLabelHorizontalAlignmentMode.
Right
```

Thanks to this change, the label will be anchored to the right of the screen, but when it becomes bigger, it will grow to the left, and, thus, we will avoid our previous problem. Time to run the game again and check out whether it worked:

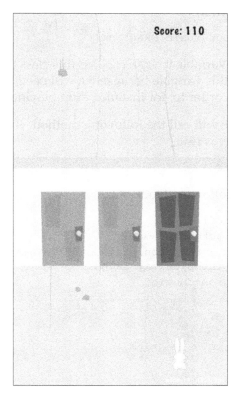

Playing some music

We all know that music is very important in films as it helps immerse viewers in the story, and this happens in video games too. Depending on the game, you will need to transmit different emotions and highlight actions or situations. Luckily, SpriteKit provides us with a group of utilities to play and handle sounds, making these tasks very simple.

Let's start by creating a new group on the project navigator and adding the needed audio resources:

- Right-click on the **InsideTheHat** group on the navigator, select **New Group**, and call it **Sound**.
- Right-click on the **Sound** group and select **Add Files to "InsideTheHat"**....
- In the `7338_02_Resources` folder, you will find `insidethehat_background.mp3`, `wrong_door.mp3`, and `correct_door.mp3`. Select them and click on **Add**.

We will start by playing the background music for our game so that it can be more interesting. We will need a variable to handle the music. Add the following line after the `score` variable declaration:

```
private var backgroundMusic:SKAction!
```

Note that the type of this variable is `SKAction`, as this class provides a way to play sound files. We declared this variable because we will need to manage it later on in the game development in order to, for instance, stop playing the background music.

To initialize the music, we will call the following method. Add the following code at the beginning of `didMoveToView`:

```
self.initializeMusic()
```

Implement this with the following block of code:

```
func initializeMusic() {
    // Initialize background music
    backgroundMusic = SKAction.playSoundFileNamed("insidethehat_
background", waitForCompletion: false)
    runAction(backgroundMusic)
}
```

In this method, we initialized the `backgroundMusic` as an `SKAction` variable. We used the `playSoundFileNamed` method, specifying the filename that we added previously to the project. One thing that needs to be highlighted is the `waitForCompletion` argument, whose value was set to `false` because in this way, the action will be completed immediately even though the sound will keep playing. If `waitForCompletion` is `true`, the duration of the action will be the same as the length of the audio file.

Finally, we have the background music. Run the game and listen to it:

Okay, if you play it for some time, you will realized that the music stops suddenly. Don't worry, this behavior was expected, as I wanted to explain a couple of things.

AVFoundation

The SpriteKit engine provides a framework called AVFoundation that allows us to handle and play audio and video resources in iOS games and apps. It provides a rich interface from which we will just take advantage of a very small part, namely the AVAudioPlayer class.

The first thing that we need to do to play sounds using this library is to add a new import to the class and paste the following line of code at the top of GameScene:

```
import AVFoundation
```

Next, we have to make a little adjustment to the backgroundMusic variable. So, replace its declaration, which looks like this:

```
private var backgroundMusic:SKAction!
```

Replace the preceding line of code with the following one:

```
private var backgroundMusic:AVAudioPlayer!
```

We have declared our variable as an instance of AVAudioPlayer, which is a class that will allow us to play sounds no matter what its duration is, make sound loops, control volumes and position the sounds in the stereo field, or play multiple sounds synchronously.

To initialize it, you will need to replace all the contents of initializeMusic with the previous block of code:

```
// Specifying the file's route in the project'
var path = NSBundle.mainBundle().pathForResource("insidethehat_
background", ofType:"mp3")
var fileURL = NSURL(fileURLWithPath: path!)

do {
    // Initialize variable
    backgroundMusic = try AVAudioPlayer(contentsOfURL: fileURL)
    // Reproduce song indefinitely
    backgroundMusic.numberOfLoops = -1
    // Play music
    backgroundMusic.play()
} catch {
    print("Error playing background music")
}
```

The first thing that we did here is create an NSURL variable by using the path to the desired resource (the audio file). The NSURL instances represent a URL that can be a file on a remote server or a file on your own device disk. So, for this purpose, we need to obtain the path to the background music file.

The NSBundle.mainBundle().pathForResource method just retrieves a string value that contains the path of the resource along with the provided name and type. In this way, we have the exact route to the desired file.

Now that we have the route to the .mp3 file, we can initialize the audio player, but, as you may have realized, it has a different look. We can encapsulate this initialization between a do { } catch statement, which is a new technique that is provided by Swift 2.0 to handle errors.

This do-catch statement is needed because, as you can see on the class reference web page at https://developer.apple.com/library/ios//documentation/AVFoundation/Reference/AVAudioPlayerClassReference/index.html#//apple_ref/occ/instm/AVAudioPlayer/initWithContentsOfURL:error:, the initializer method is marked with the throws keyword. Therefore, if you don't encapsulate the method and specify the try statement, Xcode will raise an error warning to catch the thrown error.

So, once we have initialized the audio player with the file that we want to play, we just need to specify that we want it to be played indefinitely, which is as easy as setting a negative value. Its default value is 0, which means that a unique reproduction of the sound file will be delivered.

Finally, we just need to execute the play() method of the audio player to start listening to the background file. One thing to emphasize on this last method is that it internally calls the prepareToPlay method, which preloads the audio on the buffer and can be used to improve the game's performance when it plays sounds several times.

Come on, run the game one more time, and you will see how the background music is reproduced in an unending loop.

2-star challenge: reproducing sound effects

In the previous section, you learned how to reproduce sounds in two different ways. Now, I would like to challenge you to write the code needed to reproduce a couple of sounds (wrong_door.mp3 and correct_door.mp3) when the rabbit crosses a wrong door or a correct door respectively.

Solution

I don't think that this challenge is very complicated, but I've qualified it as a 2-star challenge because you need to add code in two to three parts of the GameScene class.

I've chosen to create two new variables to handle each of the sounds. Add the following lines to the GameScene class:

```
private var wrongDoorSound: AVAudioPlayer!
private var correctDoorSound: AVAudioPlayer!
```

I declared them as the AVAudioPlayer instances as it will provide a little more efficiency due to the way I coded it.

Next, we need to declare these new variables. So, add the following block of code in the do-catch statement in the initializeMusic method just after backgroundMusic.play():

```
// Preparing wrong door sound
path = NSBundle.mainBundle().pathForResource("wrong_door",
ofType:"mp3")
fileURL = NSURL(fileURLWithPath: path!)
wrongDoorSound = try AVAudioPlayer(contentsOfURL: fileURL)
wrongDoorSound.volume = 1.0
wrongDoorSound.prepareToPlay()

// Preparing correct door sound
path = NSBundle.mainBundle().pathForResource("correct_door",
ofType:"mp3")
fileURL = NSURL(fileURLWithPath: path!)
correctDoorSound = try AVAudioPlayer(contentsOfURL: fileURL)
correctDoorSound.volume = 0.9
correctDoorSound.prepareToPlay()
```

We initialized both the variables using the same approach that was followed for the background music. We specified the route of the filename and then, we initialized the variable, but there are two new lines after that.

On the first line of code, we specified the volume variable for the sound as 1.0. This is the default value that it contains, and it indicates that we want this sound to be played with the maximum level of volume (for the correct door sound, we specify 0.9, as this file's volume is a bit loud).

Finally, we executed the `prepareToPlay` method on both the players because we want them to be ready to be triggered as soon as the rabbit collides with a wrong or a correct door in the game, thus minimizing the CPU usage taken every time it happens.

Now that we have prepared the sounds, we just need to reproduce them at the precise moment. Add the following lines in the `detectCollisions` method just after `self.isCollisionDetected = true`:

```
// Reproduce sound
self.playWrongDoorSound()
```

This will call a new method. So implement it using the following code:

```
func playWrongDoorSound() {
    // Play wrong door sound
    wrongDoorSound.play()
}
```

This method will just play the sound. A big effort was made for the initializer method, and the cost of playing the sounds will be very low.

Let's do the same thing for the `correct door` sound. Add the preceding block of code to `detectCollisions`, this time before `node.hidden = true`:

```
else {
    // Reproduce sound
    self.playCorrectDoorSound()
}
```

This code will raise an error, when a collision and the node's `name` object doesn't contain the word `wrong`. Hence, it will be called when a correct door is crossed.

Finally, implement this last method using the following lines:

```
func playCorrectDoorSound() {
    // Play correct door sound
    correctDoorSound.play()
}
```

As seen in the previous method, this one will just play the **correct door** sound in an efficient way.

Run the game one last time and check out the brand new sounds:

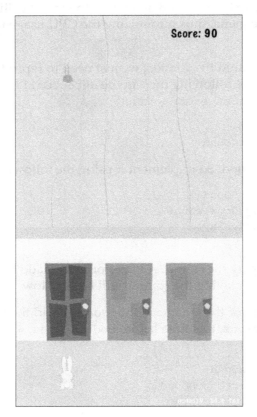

Summary

In this chapter, we focused our efforts on incorporating playability in the game that we initialized in *Chapter 1, The First Step toward SpriteKit*.

We explored the different ways through which we can handle touch interaction, and we used them to detect where the user touched the screen and deploy it on the movements of the main character.

In order to make the rabbit move, we had a look at the methods provided by the SKAction class in order to create and manage actions. Thanks to these utilities, we managed the rabbit's lateral movement and the looped movement of the wall and doors. In this way, we created a group of objects that the user will need to avoid.

Next, we added one of the bases of all games, namely collision detection. As the rabbit will need to avoid the wrong doors, we had to find a way to check whether a collision took place. So, we saw how to detect whether a collision happened and how to handle it in order to convert it into a success or failure.

We used this collision to convert it into a reward for the player, which will be shown as a score label on the view. We had a look at how to create labels easily using a font supported by iOS and use its alignment attribute in order to place the labels wherever we want.

Finally, we took advantage of two different techniques to reproduce audio files in games so that we can help players immerse in the game.

Now that we have implemented the basis of game development, in the next chapter, you will learn some advanced techniques to make your games more complex and professional.

3

Taking Games
One Step Further

In *Chapter 2*, *What Makes a Game a Game?*, we learned some techniques that are used in almost every video game. In this chapter, we will talk about some techniques that are used to add complexity to games, such as creating our own SKNode subclasses or drawing geometrical primitives. We will also learn some other techniques that will provide a realistic look and feel to a game, such as animating sprites or implementing the parallax effect.

You will learn the following things in this chapter:

- How to create classes that extend SKNode
- How to implement the parallax effect
- How to animate sprites
- Drawing geometrical primitives

Extending the SKNode class

When designing games, you may need to provide some extra behavior and complexity to sprites and nodes. For example, we may sometimes like to create nodes that consist of several sprites or develop enemies that can behave in one way or another, depending on its type.

For this purpose, one useful solution is to create customized nodes by extending SKNode in order to inherit all of its properties and utilities and building a complex class to provide the behavior needed for a game.

For the game, we are going to take advantage of this approach to load some enemies. The rabbit's escape route, which is shown in the following screenshot, is a part of the doors, and will be filled by enemies. The enemies will be puppet rabbits, which will move laterally on a rail. These enemies can be of two types. Depending on their type, they will move either from left to right, or from right to left.

Before implementing this solution, let's open the initial project for this chapter, which is very similar to how we left it at the end of *Chapter 2, What Makes a Game a Game?* However, I added some modifications just to prevent some weird behavior and code cleaning.

If you unzip 7338_03_Resources.zip, you will find InsideTheHat_init.zip. Unzip it and open the project with **Xcode**.

On the top of GameScene.swift, you will see one new flag called isMovementAllowed and a constant named kRunningSpeed, which is used to ensure that all the elements that move towards the main character have the same speed. That way, we can manage the elements by modifying just one variable.

 We are using a naming convention for constants in order to easily differentiate them from variables.

We use the previous flag (isMovementAllowed) to check whether the rabbit can be moved by adding a condition to touchesBegan, and this flag is modified when a collision happens so that no movement can be performed.

I've modified the zPosition values for the game so that it can be visually more realistic since we are going to add some other nodes.

In addition to this, I've changed the `nextPosition` value for the rabbit when it moves to the left or right side of the screen. As we want the main character to be centered at the door's position, we will use the door's horizontal value for `moveRabbitToNextLocation`.

The last change in the code is the value returned by the `supportedInterfaceOrientations` method in `GameViewController`, which will return `.Portrait` for both iPhone and iPad devices.

Creating a new class

The first thing that we need to do to add a customized enemy to the game is to create a new class. For this purpose, perform the following steps:

1. In **Xcode**, select the **File** menu at the top of the screen.

2. Browse **New** | **File**, and you will see what's shown in the following screenshot:

3. Select the **Swift File** option in **iOS | Source** and click on the **Next** button.

4. Call it **Enemy** and choose the folder where you want it to be saved before clicking on the **Create** button.

If you now open `Enemy.swift`, you will see that this file has only one code line:

```
import Foundation
```

Don't worry; we are going to add the necessary code so that the enemy appears real. Let's start by defining the class as a subclass of `SKNode`. Add the following lines at the end of the file:

```
import SpriteKit

class Enemy: SKNode {
}
```

In the preceding code, we just imported the `SpriteKit` framework and specified that the class will inherit `SKNode`.

Now, add the following block of code at the top of the class just after the imports section:

```
enum EnemyType : UInt32 {
    case ENEMY_LEFT_RIGHT = 0
    case ENEMY_RIGHT_LEFT = 1
}
```

As we are going to create two types of enemies, we will create an enumeration to support both of them: the enemies that start from the left-hand side of the screen and the others that start from the right-hand side. You can see that the type of the enumeration is `UInt32`. We chose this type in order to make the tasks easier when randomly creating enemies. Don't worry about this. Keep reading to understand it.

Now, add the following block just after `class Enemy: SKNode {`:

```
internal var rail: SKSpriteNode!
internal var puppet: SKSpriteNode!
internal var leftAction: SKAction!
internal var rightAction: SKAction!
internal var enemyType: EnemyType
```

In the preceding code, we declared two `SKSpriteNode` variables that will be used to represent the puppet and the rail respectively. We also declared two actions, which will be used to store both movements: the one that moves from left to right and the other one that moves from the right side of the screen to the left side.

Finally, we declared an `EnemyType` variable so that we can store the type of the enemy in case we need it later.

 We declared the `SKSpritenode` and `EnemyType` variables using the `internal` access level. As defined in `https://developer.apple.com/library/prerelease/ios/documentation/Swift/Conceptual/Swift_Programming_Language/AccessControl.html`, this level of access allows a class in the same module to make use of the variables. Thanks to this level of access, we will be able to access these entities from the `scene` class.

At this point, the class is raising an error warning about initializers not existing. So, let's solve it by adding the following code at the end of the `Enemy` class:

```
init(type: EnemyType) {
    // Set enemy type
    enemyType = type

    // Call parent's init method'
    super.init()

    // Initialize rail sprite
    rail = SKSpriteNode(imageNamed: "rail")

    // Initialize puppet sprite
    setPuppetTexture()

    // Add sprites to the node
    addChild(rail)
    addChild(puppet)
}
```

As you can see, we created an `init` method that expects an `EnemyType` variable as an input parameter. The first thing that we need to do in this method is to assign the type received as the `enemyType` variable of the class.

Then, we called the initializer of the parent class (SKNode). The purpose of calling it just after initializing the enemyType property is for the following two reasons:

1. If we call super.init() before all the properties have been initialized, it will raise the property not initialized at super.init call error. It isn't applicable to optional properties, like properties with a default value, or lazy properties. This is why we don't need to initialize the rest of properties beforehand.

2. We need to initialize it before the rest of the method calls, or it will raise the Use of self in method call before super.init initializes self error.

After calling the parent's initializer, we can proceed by initializing the rest of the properties. This is why we initialize the rail sprite using an image. Don't worry about this image now; we will add it to the project before running the game.

Then, we need to initialize the puppet by calling a method. The purpose of doing it this way is that we will take advantage of the enemyType property on each game's wave so that we don't need to initialize the enemy each time, and modifying its texture is enough.

Implement the setPuppetTexture method within the following block of code:

```
func setPuppetTexture() {
    switch enemyType {
    case .ENEMY_LEFT_RIGHT:
        // Initialize the puppet if nil
        if (puppet == nil) {
            puppet = SKSpriteNode(imageNamed: "enemyLeft")
        } else {
            // Update texture
            puppet.texture = SKTexture(imageNamed: "enemyLeft")
        }
        break

    case .ENEMY_RIGHT_LEFT:
        // Initialize the puppet if nil
        if (puppet == nil) {
            puppet = SKSpriteNode(imageNamed: "enemyRight")
        } else {
            // Update texture
            puppet.texture = SKTexture(imageNamed: "enemyRight")
        }
        break
    }

    puppet.anchorPoint = CGPointMake(0.5, 0.0)
}
```

This method will initialize the puppet sprite in two similar ways, depending on its type. If the enemy is the one that will start on the left side, we create a sprite. If it is null, we use the respective image name and, in case the sprite already exists, we just modify its texture.

Finally, we set the `anchorPoint` value of the puppet so that when we add it to the node, its bottom coincides with the center of the rail, achieving the expected result.

Once both the sprites have been initialized, we can add them to the node, and we will have the new object formed by two different images.

Before going further, let's add the necessary images to the **Xcode** project. To achieve this purpose, perform the following steps:

1. Right-click on **Art** and select **Add Files to InsideTheHat...**.

2. You'll find `rail.png`, `enemyLeft.png`, `enemyRight.png`, `rail@2x.png`, `enemyLeft@2x.png`, `enemyRight@2x.png`, `rail@2x~ipad.png`, `enemyLeft@2x~ipad.png`, `enemyRight@2x~ipad.png`, `rail@3x.png`, `enemyLeft@3x.png`, and `enemyRight@3x.png` in the `7338_03_Resources` folder that you unzipped previously. Select these 12 files and click on **Add**.

Now that we have finished writing the code for the `custom` class, you will realize that there is still an error that warns us by stating that `required initializer init(coder:) must be provided by subclass of SKNode`. The initializer method that it asks for (`init(coder:)`) is a way to declare to the compiler that we are not expecting the class to be *NSCoding-compatible*, which means that we are not going to serialize or deserialize the class instances.

To solve this error, you can just click on the red circle with a white circle inside it and accept the proposed fix, which will add the following code to the class:

```
required init?(coder aDecoder: NSCoder) {
    fatalError("init(coder:) has not been implemented")
}
```

Okay, it's time to add the enemies to the scene.

Handling the behavior of custom classes

We have built a complex object that was formed by two different sprites. But now, we want them to work as a unique body. With each wave, the rail and the puppet will perform a vertical movement that is similar to that of the doors and the wall and, in addition to this, the puppet will need to perform a lateral movement from left to right or vice versa, depending on the enemy's type. This is shown in the following screenshot:

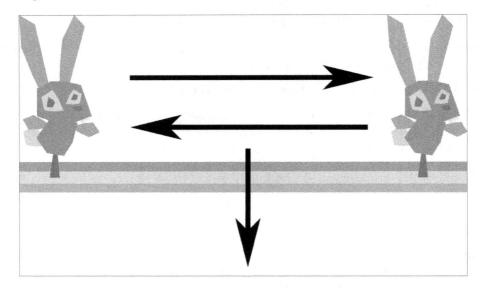

To understand the provided specifications, we will need to create different actions and run them separately on the sprites that are a part of the enemy node.

Let's start by adding the enemy to the scene. For this purpose, we will need to declare a new variable. Add the following line to the top of the GameScene implementation:

```
private var enemy: Enemy!
```

By using this line, we declare an instance of the customized class.

 We are not importing the Enemy class, because in the Swift programming language, it is no longer needed.

Now, add the following method call at the end of `didMoveToView`:

```
self.initializeEnemy()
```

Implement this method by adding the following block of code to `GameScene`:

```
func initializeEnemy() {
    // Create enemy type
    let enemyType: EnemyType = EnemyType(rawValue: arc4random_
uniform(2))!

    // Initialize the enemy with type
    enemy = Enemy(type: enemyType)

    // Specify zPosition values
    enemy.rail.zPosition = 0
    enemy.puppet.zPosition = 1

    // Set initial position
    enemy.position = CGPoint(x: (view!.bounds.size.width/2), y: view!.
bounds.size.height/2)

    // Add enemy to the scene
    addChild(enemy)
}
```

In the first line, we initialized a constant with a random enemy type. As you can see, we can initialize the enumerated type by calling its `init` method and passing a `rawValue` variable as an input parameter. In this way, we create a random value between `0` and `1` that we will use to initialize the enemy's type.

You may remember that we declared the enumerated values as `UInt32` because the type of the value returned by the `arc4random_uniform` method is a `UInt32` value.

Once we created the type, we called the `init` method of the custom class that will internally initialize the sprite nodes, depending on the type.

Then, we specified the `zPosition` values for both the `rail` and `puppet` sprites so that they are placed in the correct depth position.

Finally, we set the enemy's position at the center of the screen and we added it to the scene. If you run the game now, you will see something that is similar to the following screenshot:

As you can see, the enemy is correctly placed at the center of the view, but what we really want is that it moves vertically and laterally, starting from the top of the view. Let's fix the initial position. You need to replace the following line:

```
enemy.position = CGPoint(x:(view!.bounds.size.width/2), y: view!.
bounds.size.height/2)
```

Add the following block of code after replacing previous code:

```
enemy.rail.position = CGPoint(x:(view!.bounds.size.width/2), y: view!.
bounds.size.height + wall.frame.size.height/2)

    switch enemyType {
        case .ENEMY_LEFT_RIGHT:
            // Set enemy's position
            enemy.puppet.position = CGPoint(x:leftDoor.position.x, y:
view!.bounds.size.height + wall.frame.size.height/2)
        break

        case .ENEMY_RIGHT_LEFT:
            // Set enemy's position
            enemy.puppet.position = CGPoint(x:rightDoor.position.x, y:
view!.bounds.size.height + wall.frame.size.height/2)
        break
    }
```

In the first line, we specified that we want the rail sprite to be at the center of the screen, but outside, we want it to be centered with the wall's initial position.

Then, we used a `switch` statement to specify the puppet's position, depending on the enemy's type. If enemy type is ENEMY_LEFT_RIGHT, we will place it at the center to the left door and out of view, centered with the wall's initial position. If the type of the enemy is the opposite, ENEMY_RIGHT_LEFT, we will place it centered with the right door.

Now that we have the initial positions correctly specified, it's time to make the enemy move. So for this purpose, we will need to call a new method. Add the following lines at the end of `initializeEnemy`:

```
// Initialize enemy's actions
initializeEnemyActions()
```

Let's implement this new method by using the following code:

```
func initializeEnemyActions() {
    // Enemy's lateral speed
    let enemyLateralSpeed: CGFloat = 150.0

    // Initialize enemy's type
    var enemyType: EnemyType = .ENEMY_LEFT_RIGHT

    // Sprite's actions
    var verticalMovementAction: SKAction!
```

```
    var lateralMovementAction: SKAction!

    // Setting the rail's final position
    let nextRailPosition = CGPoint(x: enemy.rail.position.x, y: -wall.
frame.size.height / 2)
    // We want the rail to move on a constant speed
    let railDuration = self.distanceBetween(point: enemy.rail.
position, andPoint: nextRailPosition) / self.kRunningSpeed
    // Move the rail to the next position
    let moveRailAction = SKAction.moveToY(nextRailPosition.y,
duration: Double(railDuration))
    }
```

We began by declaring a constant variable that will be used to specify the speed of the lateral movement so that the puppet moves lineally.

Then, we declared a variable for the enemy's type with a default value, and we also declared two different actions: one for the vertical movement and another one for the lateral movement.

To create the vertical movement, we are going to take the rail as a reference. We specified the final position, which is the same place as that on the x coordinate but the opposite on the y coordinate. This way, the enemy will finish its vertical movement outside the screen, but at the bottom of the view this time.

When we declared the duration for this vertical movement. For this purpose, we need the distance between the rail sprite and the final position. We also used the kRunningSpeed constant for this movement as we want it to be similar to the wall's and the door's constant.

Finally, we declared a moveToY action to specify the already-calculated final position and the duration.

Once the enemy arrives at the final position, we need it to recover its initial location. So, let's add another action for this purpose by adding the following lines at the end of initializeEnemyActions:

```
    // Reset the rail's position
    let resetPositionAction = SKAction.runBlock {
        // Reset rail's position
        self.enemy.rail.position = CGPoint(x:self.view!.bounds.size.
width/2, y: self.view!.bounds.size.height + self.wall.frame.size.
height/2)

        // Reset enemy's type
        enemyType = EnemyType(rawValue: arc4random_uniform(2))!
```

```
        self.enemy.enemyType = enemyType

        // Stop previous action
        self.enemy.puppet.removeActionForKey("puppet_action")

        switch enemyType {
            case .ENEMY_LEFT_RIGHT:
                // Reset texture
                self.enemy.setPuppetTexture()
                // Reset position
                self.enemy.puppet.position = CGPoint(x:self.leftDoor.
position.x, y: self.view!.bounds.size.height + self.wall.frame.size.
height/2)

                // Run action
                self.enemy.puppet.runAction(SKAction.
repeatActionForever(self.enemy.leftAction), withKey: "puppet_action")
            break

            case .ENEMY_RIGHT_LEFT:
                // Reset texture
                self.enemy.setPuppetTexture()
                // Reset position
                self.enemy.puppet.position = CGPoint(x:self.rightDoor.
position.x, y: self.view!.bounds.size.height + self.wall.frame.size.
height/2)

                // Run action
                self.enemy.puppet.runAction(SKAction.
repeatActionForever(self.enemy.rightAction), withKey: "puppet_action")
            break
        }
    }
```

Don't worry if this piece of code is bigger than the usual; we are combining different techniques that we have been using on other actions, and you will easily understand it.

We began by creating a `runBlock` action so that we can execute all the steps needed to recover the initial status. The first thing is to reset the rail's position, as it will be different to that of the puppet. Also, as you can see, we specified the same point as that of the initial position.

Then, we reset the enemy's type by calling the `init` method again. Then, we set it to the enemy's node. This way, each wave of enemies will be randomly created.

As we are going to execute a vertical and a lateral action on the puppet (the rail will only run the vertical action), we need a way to stop any previous lateral action. This is why we execute the removeActionForKey method for the puppet node, specifying the puppet_action key.

Once we are sure that there will not be repeated actions, we will take advantage of the switch statement to reset some puppet's attributes, depending on its type. As you can see, we called the setPuppetTexture method in order to update the sprite texture, but it will not create a new node each time; it will just update the texture.

Then, we reset the puppet's position by placing it at its original point. Then, we run the leftAction or the rightAction variables on the puppet sprite, giving it the same key name that we previously used to stop actions.

At this very moment, the leftAction or rightAction variables aren't yet created. But let's continue implementing the method, and everything will make sense.

Add the following block of code at the end of initializeEnemyActions:

```
// Delay action
let delayAction = SKAction.waitForDuration(2.0)

// Creating sequence of actions
let railSequence = SKAction.sequence([delayAction, moveRailAction,
resetPositionAction])

// Initializing vertical movement action
verticalMovementAction = SKAction.repeatActionForever(railSequence)

// We want the puppet to move on a constant speed
let puppetDuration = self.distanceBetween(point: rightDoor.position,
andPoint: leftDoor.position) / enemyLateralSpeed

// Initialize lateral actions
let moveEnemyLeftAction = SKAction.moveToX(leftDoor.position.x,
duration: Double(puppetDuration))
let moveEnemyRightAction = SKAction.moveToX(rightDoor.position.x,
duration: Double(puppetDuration))

// Initialize sequence of actions
enemy.leftAction = SKAction.sequence([moveEnemyRightAction,
moveEnemyLeftAction])
enemy.rightAction = SKAction.sequence([moveEnemyLeftAction,
moveEnemyRightAction])
```

We will need a delay action because we want the enemy to move a little further from the wall and doors so that there is a short distance between them. This is why we created a `waitForDuration` action with a value of 2 seconds.

Now that we have all the actions needed for the rail to behave as we want, we created a sequence with the delay, the rail movement, and the reset action, and we use this sequence to initialize the `verticalMovementAction` object, which will repeat the sequence in an endless loop.

Now that the vertical movement is done, we defined the puppets actions. This is why we first calculated the duration of the lateral movement between the left and right sides of the screen. Note how we specified the left and right doors as the points at which motion reverses the distance because the movements will reach each of those extremes.

With this duration, we initialized two lateral movements: one for the puppet to move from left to right and another one for the puppet to move from right to left. Finally, we used both actions to create a sequence in order to initialize `leftAction` and `rightAction` objects. In this way, when we execute the `resetPositionAction` object, we just need to execute the corresponding actions to achieve the desired movement.

We are almost finished with the coding for the enemy's actions; just add the following lines at the end of `initializeEnemyActions`:

```
switch enemy.enemyType {
    case .ENEMY_LEFT_RIGHT:
        // Initializing puppet's action
        lateralMovementAction = SKAction.repeatActionForever(enemy.
leftAction)
    break

    case .ENEMY_RIGHT_LEFT:
        // Initializing puppet's action
        lateralMovementAction = SKAction.repeatActionForever(enemy.
rightAction)
      break
}

    // Running vertical movement actions
    enemy.rail.runAction(verticalMovementAction)
    enemy.puppet.runAction(verticalMovementAction)

    // Running lateral movement action
    enemy.puppet.runAction(lateralMovementAction, withKey: "puppet_
action")
```

Now that we have all the desired actions, we take advantage of a `switch` statement again to initialize the `lateralMovementAction` variable, which will run the left or right action respectively, depending on the enemy's type in an endless loop.

Then, as everything is ready, we can run the `verticalMovementAction` object on both the rail and puppet sprites so that they can move vertically and the `lateralMovementAction` object of the puppet node, specifying a key name.

After performing all of these tasks, it's time to check what we have done. So, run the game again, and you will see the enemy moving as expected:

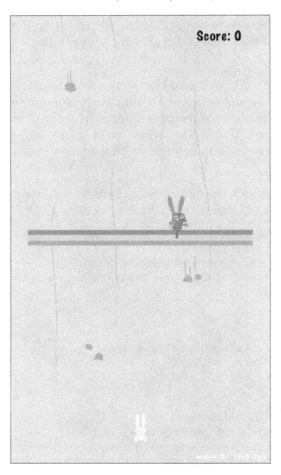

2-star challenge: colliding puppets

Before going further, you need to add the code that detect collisions between the
rabbit and the puppet. When this happens, the blinking action should be run as well
as the sound that is played when the rabbit collides with the wrong door. Also, you
should take into account that colliding with the enemies will not affect the score.

Solution

I've decided to use a different flag to detect whether a collision with an enemy
happened, as we will need it later in this chapter. So, let's add a new variable
declaration at the top of GameScene:

```
private var isEnemyCollisionDetected: Bool = false
```

Then, we need to write the code that detects these collisions. So, add the following
block of code at the end of detectCollisions:

```
// Check puppet collision
if enemy.puppet.frame.intersects(rabbit.frame) && (enemy.puppet.
position.y - enemy.puppet.frame.height/2) <= rabbit.position.y {

    // Collision detected
    isEnemyCollisionDetected = true

    // Reproduce sound
    self.playWrongDoorSound()

    // Make the rabbit blink
    let blinkAction = SKAction.sequence([
    SKAction.colorizeWithColor(UIColor.redColor(), colorBlendFactor:
0.5, duration: 0.1),
        SKAction.fadeAlphaTo(0.0, duration: 0.2),
        SKAction.fadeAlphaTo(1.0, duration: 0.2),
        SKAction.colorizeWithColor(UIColor.whiteColor(),
colorBlendFactor: 1.0, duration: 0.1)      ])
    self.rabbit.runAction(SKAction.repeatAction(blinkAction, count:
3))
}
```

As we just want to detect the collisions with the puppet, we need to check whether
the puppet's frame intersects the rabbit's frame. Note that we also added a condition
to make this detection more accurate.

If a collision happens, we need to update the flag and play a sound (we use the same sound as we used for the wrong door). Finally, we need to run the same blink action that we run when the rabbit collides with the wrong door.

We just need to reset the flag's value when the enemy finishes its movement. So, add the following lines to `initializeEnemyActions` at the beginning of `let resetPositionAction = SKAction.runBlock {`:

```
// Reset flag
self.isEnemyCollisionDetected = false
```

If you run the game now, you will see how the rabbit will collide with the doors and the puppets too, as shown in the following screenshot:

The parallax effect

When developing two-dimensional games, you will come across a problem that traditional animators have been facing since the development of the cartoon, which is the difficulty of providing their creations with depth and the sensation of motion.

The technique used by animators to solve this problem is the one known as **parallax effect**, which involves the separation of scenes onto different layers and moving the background ones slower than the layers in the foreground.

This is something that is similar to what happens when you are traveling in an automobile. If you look at one side, you will see trees on the edge of the road passing by swiftly. If you then look a little further at a static object, you will see that it moves slower than the trees. Furthermore, if you look at the horizon, you will see that mountains almost seem static.

By applying the parallax effect, we make our brain think that there is depth in the scene (we achieve a three-dimensional effect) and movement is happening, but the reality is that the different layers are moving at different speeds while being placed on the same plane.

To apply this technique to our game, we will take an approach that involves moving the background and some lateral trees from the top to the bottom in a way that is similar to how we moved the walls, doors, and enemies.

If we move the background, then we will find a problem that the background disappears from the scene and a blank layer will be kept as a background for the game. In order to avoid this problem, we will place a background copy on top of the original one to constantly cover the view.

We will also apply the same duplication to the trees on both sides of the road so that we can move them with a speed that is different sides that of the background. In this way, we will simulate that the rabbit is running. This is shown in the following screenshot:

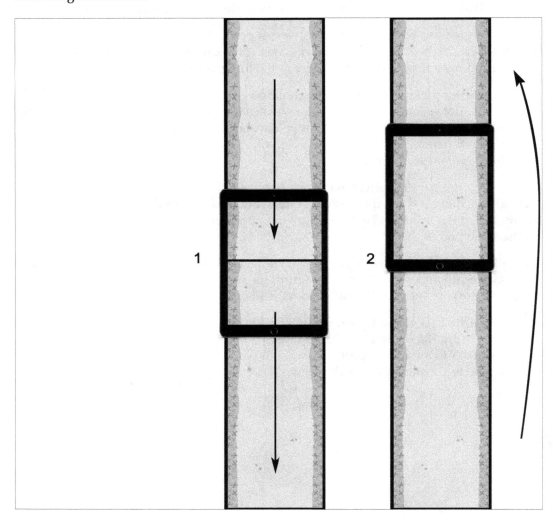

Okay, now that the concept is clear and we have planned what we are going to implement, let's start by adding the parallax layers to the scene: the backgrounds and the trees.

First of all, we need to remove the background that we added to the scene in *Chapter 1, The First Step toward SpriteKit*. Hence, remove the following lines from `initializeMainCharacter`:

```
// Creating and adding the background to the scene
let background = SKSpriteNode(imageNamed: "background")
background.anchorPoint = .zero
background.zPosition = -1


addChild(background)
```

Furthermore, let's declare some variables that will be useful for the development of the parallax effect. Add the following lines just after `private var isEnemyCollisionDetected: Bool = false`:

```
private var backgroundBottom: SKSpriteNode!
private var backgroundTop: SKSpriteNode!
private var treesBottom: SKSpriteNode!
private var treesTop: SKSpriteNode!
```

To initialize these variables, we are going to call a new method. Add the following line at the end of `didMoveToView`:

```
self.initializeParallaxEffect()
```

Implement this with the following lines of code:

```
func initializeParallaxEffect() {
    // Initialize background layers
    backgroundBottom = SKSpriteNode(imageNamed: "background")
    backgroundBottom.anchorPoint = .zero
    backgroundBottom.zPosition = -1

    // Copy the previous node into another
    backgroundTop = backgroundBottom.copy() as! SKSpriteNode
    // Set top layer position
    backgroundTop.position = CGPoint(x: backgroundBottom.position.x,
y: backgroundBottom.position.y + backgroundBottom.size.height)

    // Initialize tree layers
    treesBottom = SKSpriteNode(imageNamed: "trees")
    treesBottom.zPosition = 4
    treesBottom.position = CGPoint(x:(view!.bounds.size.width/2), y:
view!.bounds.size.height/2)
```

```
    // Copy the previous node into another
    treesTop = treesBottom.copy() as! SKSpriteNode
    // Set top layer position
    treesTop.position = CGPoint(x: treesBottom.position.x, y:
treesBottom.position.y + treesBottom.size.height)

    // Add background layers to the scene
    addChild(backgroundBottom)
    addChild(backgroundTop)

    // Add tree layers to the scene
    addChild(treesBottom)
    addChild(treesTop)
}
```

We first initialized `backgroundBottom` in a way that is the same as how we initialized the static background that we created in *Chapter 1, The First Step toward SpriteKit*. As you can see, we specified the `.zero` value as `anchorPoint` and placed it at the deepest `zPosition` value of the scene.

Then, we created `backgroundTop` as a copy of the previous one. As you can see, we used the `copy()` method, which is inherited from the `NSObject` class (the parent of `SKNode`), and it returns an exact copy of the previous node.

> We specified that we want the node copy to be an instance of `SKSpriteNode`, as the `copy()` method creates an object with no specific type.

Thanks to this method, we don't need to set the `anchorPoint` nor the `zPosition` values, we just need to specify the position that we want the top background to take. As we want it to be placed at the top of the bottom background, we set its *y* coordinate's position as the sum of the background and its height.

Then, we initialized both the top and bottom trees in a similar way we used for the backgrounds. We first created one of the nodes using the `"trees"` texture and specified its `zPosition` object so that the result makes sense. We also set its position so that it is centered on the screen. Finally, we created a copy of the previous node, specifying its particular position.

Before running the game, let's add to the project the images that we used to create the trees by performing the following steps:

1. Right-click on **Art** and select **Add Files to "InsideTheHat"**....

2. You'll find `trees.png`, `trees@2x.png`, `trees@2x~ipad.png`, and `trees@3x.png` in the `7338_03_Resources` folder that you previously unzipped. Select these four files and click on **Add**.

Finally, add the four nodes to the scene so that they are ready to start running the parallax effect. Execute the project now and have a look at what we have done so far:

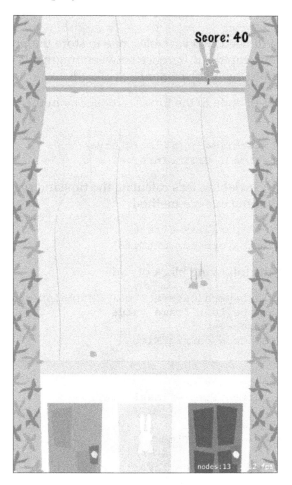

Now that we have all the necessary elements, it's time to start running the parallax effect. For this purpose, we can take advantage of the already-known actions and make the different layers move from top to bottom with different speeds, but we are going to use a different approach this time.

The update method and delta times

You may remember that the update method receives a CFTimeInterval value, which is the interval of the time where the current frame is placed. We can use this fragment of time to calculate the displacement that the different layers will perform for each frame.

For this purpose, we will need two variables: one to store the previous interval of time and another one to keep the difference between fragments of time (delta) in order to use it to calculate the displacement.

Add the following lines of code to the top of GameScene in the variable declaration section:

```
private var lastFrameTime : CFTimeInterval = 0
private var deltaTime : CFTimeInterval = 0
```

Now that we have both variables, let's calculate the time intervals. Add the following method call at the end of the update method:

```
// Update layers on parallax effect
self.updateParallaxLayers(currentTime)
```

Implement this using the following block of code:

```
func updateParallaxLayers(currentTime: CFTimeInterval) {
    // Initialize the last frame value
    if lastFrameTime <= 0 {
        lastFrameTime = currentTime
    }

    // Update the delta time
    deltaTime = currentTime - lastFrameTime

    // Update the last frame time
    lastFrameTime = currentTime

    // Apply the delta to the layer's position
    self.moveParallaxLayer(backgroundBottom, topLayer:backgroundTop,
speed:kBackgroundSpeed)
    self.moveParallaxLayer(treesBottom, topLayer:treesTop,
speed:kTreesSpeed)
}
```

As you can see, we are sending the `currentTime` value as an input parameter to the method, as we will need it to calculate the delta times.

The first thing that we do in this method is initialize the `lastFrameTime` variable with the current time. This value will be used to calculate the difference between the last time and the current one (`deltaTime`), but on the first call to the method, the delta value will be `0`.

Then, we store the current time as the last time so that we have this reference to calculate the following delta values.

Once we have performed this calculation, we call the `moveParallaxLayer` method, where we will apply the delta value for both the layers, namely backgrounds and trees, specifying the different speeds that we want them to have. As you can see, we are using two new constant values (`kBackgroundSpeed` and `kTreesSpeed`). Add them to the top of the class:

```
private let kBackgroundSpeed: CGFloat = 250.0
    private let kTreesSpeed: CGFloat = 450.0
```

Finally, let's implement this last `moveParallaxLayer` method:

```
func moveParallaxLayer(bottomLayer : SKSpriteNode, topLayer :
SKSpriteNode, speed : CGFloat) -> Void {
    // Initialize next position
    var nextPosition = CGPointZero

    for parallaxLayer in [bottomLayer, topLayer] {
        // Update next position
        nextPosition = parallaxLayer.position
        nextPosition.y -= CGFloat(speed * CGFloat(deltaTime))
        // Update layer position
        parallaxLayer.position = nextPosition

        // If the layer is out of view
        if parallaxLayer.frame.maxY < self.frame.minY {
            // Reset layer position
            parallaxLayer.position =
CGPoint(x: parallaxLayer.position.x, y: parallaxLayer.position.y +
parallaxLayer.size.height * 2)
        }
    }
}
```

This method receives both layers, the top and the bottom, that are a part of the parallax nodes and the speed at which we want them to move.

First of all, we initialized a variable. We are going to keep the next position. We want the layers to move to and fro. With a loop, we can iterate the bottom and top layers.

For each variable, we initialize the next position so that we can keep the x coordinate as the original one. Then, we calculate the y position. We calculated this value by multiplying the delta factor that we got on previous step and speed one less then the previous step.

This way, the difference in the position will be very small. Hence, the movement result will be smooth enough. Then, we will use this new position value to update the layer's position.

The last past of the method checks whether the layer's frame is completely out of sight. For this purpose, we check whether the maximum value in the y coordinate of the layer's frame is lower than the minimum value of the view's frame.

If this is the case, we need to restore the initial value. So, we place the rabbit at its initial position.

With the preceding code, we implemented the parallax effect. Now, it's time to run the game and check how it looks like:

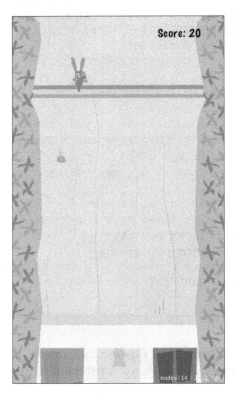

Creating animations in SpriteKit

Until this point, we have given movement to almost every node in the scene in order to make our game look realistic, but we still have our main character static and it doesn't look very normal. It looks as if the rabbit is floating over the ground.

In order to overcome this situation, we are going to animate the rabbit so that it appears as if it is running or jumping through the doors. Animating nodes consists of intercalating images with a little modification in relation to the previous one so that their visualization provides a simulation of movement.

The problem that this technique can produce is that the performance of the game can suffer alarmingly due to the large amount of images needed. To avoid this issue, we can take advantage of **texture atlases**, which are collections of images that contain all the images, thus reducing the number of draw calls.

In SpriteKit, we can create atlases easily by collecting all the necessary textures in a folder with the .atlas suffix.

So, let's start by adding an atlas to the game by following these instructions:

1. Right-click on **Art** and select **Add Files to "InsideTheHat"...**.
2. You'll find AnimationsImages.atlas in the 7338_03_Resources folder that you previously unzipped. Select it and click on **Add**.

This bundle of images contains the textures that are needed to create two animations: one for the rabbit jumping and another one for the rabbit when it collides with the wrong door or some enemy.

Now, you should ask yourself, how do we create animations in SpriteKit? Keep reading, and you will get the answer.

To create animations, we first need an array with the images that we are going to use. So, let's add a couple of variables and constants. Paste the following lines at the top of GameScene:

```
private var jumpingRabbitFrames : [SKTexture]!
private var smashingRabbitFrames : [SKTexture]!
private let kNumJumpTextures = 11
private let kNumSmashTextures = 11
```

We declared two different arrays, one for each of the animations that we are going to run, and two constants for the number of textures that take part in each action.

Then, we call the method that will initialize the animations. So, add the following line at the end of the `didMoveToView` method:

```
self.initializeAnimations()
```

Implement this using the following block of code:

```
func initializeAnimations() {
    // Reference for the atlas
    let animationsAtlas = SKTextureAtlas(named: "AnimationsImages")
    // Initialize arrays
    var auxJumpFrames = [SKTexture]()
    var auxSmashFrames = [SKTexture]()
    // Variable for the textures
    var jumpTexture: String
    var smashTexture: String

    for var i = 1; i <= kNumJumpTextures; i++ {
        // Get the corresponding texture
        jumpTexture = "rabbitJump\(i)"
        // Add texture to the array
        auxJumpFrames.append(animationsAtlas.
textureNamed(jumpTexture))
    }

    for var i = 1; i <= kNumSmashTextures; i++ {
        // Get the corresponding texture
        smashTexture = "rabbitSmash\(i)"
        // Add texture to the array
        auxSmashFrames.append(animationsAtlas.
textureNamed(smashTexture))
    }

    // Initialize the array of textures
    jumpingRabbitFrames = auxJumpFrames
    smashingRabbitFrames = auxSmashFrames
}
```

The first thing that we do in the method is create a `SKTextureAtlas` variable that will reference the texture atlas.

Then, we declare a couple of auxiliary texture arrays and a couple of variables to store the different image names that we will get from the atlas.

With a loop, we iterate all the textures for the jump animation (which is why we declare the kNumJumpTextures and kNumSmashTextures constants). We prepare each texture name, as we have decided to call them rabbitJump1 to rabbitJump11, and we use this name to retrieve it from the atlas. Finally, with this image, we update the array of textures.

 To retrieve each texture, we just need to call the textureNamed method with the required file name.

We perform the same actions in a different loop for the smash animation. Then, we update the two arrays with the auxiliary ones.

Now that we have the textures ready, let's start animating the rabbit. For this purpose, add the following line at the end of the didMoveToView method:

```
self.startJumpingRabbit()
```

Implement it using the following block of code:

```
func startJumpingRabbit() {
    // Run jumping animation
    rabbit.runAction(SKAction.repeatActionForever(SKAction.animateW
ithTextures(jumpingRabbitFrames, timePerFrame: 0.05, resize: false,
restore: true)), withKey:"jumping_rabbit")
}
```

As you can see, we are performing the action in just one line, in which we run an unending action with a key so that we can identify it later. The action that we run is animateWithTextures. We pass the array of frames that we built in the previous step to this action, identifying the time per frame.

This attribute specifies the time each texture will be viewed and can be modified. I've specified 0.05 in order to make the animation related to the parallax speed.

We can also specify whether we want each texture to be resized in order to match the previous one. We can also specify that we want to restore the texture to the first one so that each loop performs smoothly.

Check out what the new animation looks like by running the project now:

2-star challenge: animate collisions

Now that we have all the elements needed to create the animation for the rabbit when it collides with the wrong door, I challenge you to use your knowledge to stop the jumping animation and run the smashing one. Don't forget to restart the jumping animation after the smashing animation has finished.

Solution

For this challenge, we will need to remove the blink action that we created in *Chapter 2, What Makes a Game a Game?*, and the one that we created for the collision between the rabbit and the puppet so that we can run the new animation instead. You need to replace the following lines of code in the `detectCollisions` method:

```
// Make the rabbit blink
let blinkAction = SKAction.sequence([
    SKAction.colorizeWithColor(UIColor.redColor(), colorBlendFactor:
0.5, duration: 0.1),
    SKAction.fadeAlphaTo(0.0, duration: 0.2),
    SKAction.fadeAlphaTo(1.0, duration: 0.2),
    SKAction.colorizeWithColor(UIColor.whiteColor(), colorBlendFactor:
1.0, duration: 0.1)])
self.rabbit.runAction(SKAction.repeatAction(blinkAction, count: 3))
```

These lines need to be replaced by the following lines of code:

```
// Stop jumping animation
self.rabbit.removeActionForKey("jumping_rabbit")
// Run smashing animation
self.startSmashingRabbit()
```

With these lines, we first stop the jumping animation to avoid mixing actions, and then we call a new method. Let's implement it by adding the following block of code:

```
func startSmashingRabbit() {
    // Create smashing animation
    let smashingRabbitAnimation = SKAction.animateWithTextures(smashin
gRabbitFrames,
    timePerFrame: 0.05,
    resize: false,
    restore: true)
    // Action to restart the jumping action
    let resetJumpingAnimation = SKAction.runBlock {
        self.startJumpingRabbit()
    }
    // Create sequence with the desired actions
    let sequence = SKAction.sequence([smashingRabbitAnimation,
resetJumpingAnimation])
    // Run the sequence
    rabbit.runAction(sequence)
}
```

In this method, we create an action to run the smashing animation. For this purpose, we use the array that contains the textures for this animation, which were created previously, and we specify the same `timePerFrame`, `resize`, and `restore` values than we used in the jumping animation.

As we want to restart the jumping animation just when the collision finishes, we create a `runBlock` action, where we will call the `startJumpingRabbit()` method.

Then, we create a sequence with both actions, and we run it on the rabbit node. If you execute the game now, you will see how it works perfectly when the main character collides with the wrong door:

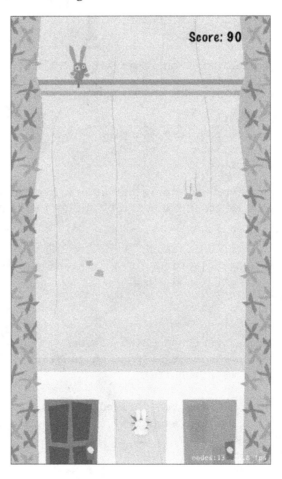

Geometrical primitives

When developing games, you will usually work with high-level elements, such as sprites, labels, particle systems, or physical bodies. But sometimes you will need to create simple shapes, such as circles, lines, rectangles. For example, you may need to do so to create a prototype for your next game.

SpriteKit provides us with a subclass of SKNode named SKShapeNode, which doesn't have much potential. This class allows us to create rectangles (init(rect:), init(rectOfSize:), init(rect:cornerRadius:), and init(rectOfSize:corne rRadius:)), ellipses (init(ellipseOfSize:) and init(ellipseInRect)), circles (init(circleOfRadius:)), and other types of shape by providing its vertices (init(points:count:)) or path (init(path:centered:)).

In this section, we are going to take advantage of this class in order to create a life bar, which will consist of a red rectangle in the background and a green rectangle in the foreground. This life bar will represent the main character's life points, and they will decrease when we collide with an enemy.

Let's start by creating the life bar. We will need to declare two new variables at the top of GameScene, as follows:

```
private var redLifeBar: SKShapeNode!
private var greenLifeBar: SKShapeNode!
```

To initialize them, we will call a new method. Add the following line at the end of didMoveToView:

```
self.initializeLifeBar()
```

Implement it using the following block of code:

```
func initializeLifeBar() {
    // Initialize red bar
    redLifeBar = SKShapeNode(rectOfSize: CGSize(width: self.view!.
bounds.width/2, height: 20.0))
    // Set bar's position
    redLifeBar.position.x = redLifeBar.frame.size.width/2 + 20
    redLifeBar.position.y = labelScore.position.y + labelScore.frame.
size.height/2
    // No border
    redLifeBar.lineWidth = 0
    // Specify zPosition
    redLifeBar.zPosition = 5
    // Set bar color
    redLifeBar.fillColor = UIColor.redColor()
}
```

We first create a new shape from a rectangle with a specified width and height. I've chosen the same size, as given in the preceding code, in order to cover the gap to the left of the score label. Then, we set the shape's *x* and *y* position in order to place it at the same level as that of the score label.

 When specifying the shape's position, it's important to know that they don't have `anchorPoint` available. Hence, its position will correspond to the center point of the shape.

We don't want the rectangle to have a border. So, we will specify this value as 0 (the default value is 1). Then, we set the shape's `zPosition` to ensure that it will remain at the top of the rest of the nodes.

Finally, we fill the shape with the desired color, which is red in this case.

Now that the red rectangle has been created, we need to create the green one. Add the following code at the end of `initializeLifeBar`:

```
// Initialize green bar
greenLifeBar = SKShapeNode(rectOfSize: CGSize(width: self.
view!.bounds.width/2, height: 20.0))
// Set bar's position
greenLifeBar.position.x = redLifeBar.position.x
greenLifeBar.position.y = redLifeBar.position.y
// No border
greenLifeBar.lineWidth = 0
// Specify zPosition
greenLifeBar.zPosition = 5
// Set bar color
greenLifeBar.fillColor = UIColor.greenColor()

// Add bars to the scene
addChild(redLifeBar)
addChild(greenLifeBar)
```

As you can see, we have initialized the green bar in the same way we initialized the red bar. We took the red rectangle as a reference for the position, and we specified green as the desired color.

Finally, we add these new nodes to the scene, as follows:

Now that the life bar is ready, we want it to decrease each time the rabbit collides with an enemy. For this purpose, we will need to know the initial life points and a variable to handle the remaining ones. Therefore, add the following lines at the top of GameScene:

```
private let kMaxNumLifePoints = 10
private var lifePoints: Int = 0
```

We declared a constant with the maximum number of life points (the initial value) and a variable that we will use to store the rabbit's life points.

To initialize this variable, add the following lines at the top of `initializeLifeBar`:

```
// Initialize life points
lifePoints = kMaxNumLifePoints
```

Now, we need to update the life bar when a puppet collides with the main character. So, add the following lines to the `initializeEnemyActions` method just after `let resetPositionAction = SKAction.runBlock {`:

```
// If the rabbit collides with the enemy
if self.isEnemyCollisionDetected {
    self.lifePoints--
    self.updateLifeBar()
}
```

When the rabbit collides with a puppet, we decrease the number of life points, and then, we call a new method. Let's implement it, and you will understand what it does:

```
func updateLifeBar() {
    // Previous bar's position
    let lastPosition = greenLifeBar.position.x
    // Previous bar's width
    let lastWidth = greenLifeBar.frame.width
    // Size of lost life
    let lostLife = redLifeBar.frame.width/CGFloat(kMaxNumLifePoints)

    // Delete previous green bar
    greenLifeBar.removeFromParent()
    // Initialize new green bar
    greenLifeBar = SKShapeNode(rectOfSize: CGSize(width: lastWidth -
lostLife, height: 20.0))
    // Set bar position
    greenLifeBar.position.x = lastPosition - lostLife/2
    greenLifeBar.position.y = redLifeBar.position.y
    // No border
    greenLifeBar.lineWidth = 0
    // Specify zPosition
    greenLifeBar.zPosition = 5
    // Set bar color
    greenLifeBar.fillColor = UIColor.greenColor()

    // Add bar to the scene
    addChild(greenLifeBar)
}
```

In this method, we are going to decrease the green bar's width to represent that we have been hit and we will need to set its position again to keep the shape immobile to the left.

For this purpose, we will obtain the green bar's previous position and width in two variables. We also initialize a constant with the width of each life point that we lost.

Then, we need to remove the previous bar and create a new one with the new width, which is the result of removing a life point from the previous width.

We need to set the new x position by removing half of the lost width, as the rectangle will decrease from both sides due to its anchor point position.

Then, we set the rest of properties as we did when initializing red and green bar, and we add the new bar to the scene. If we run the game now, we will see how it behaves. Don't worry if the life bar acts weirdly when losing all the points, as we will correct it in *Chapter 4, From the Basics to Professional Games*:

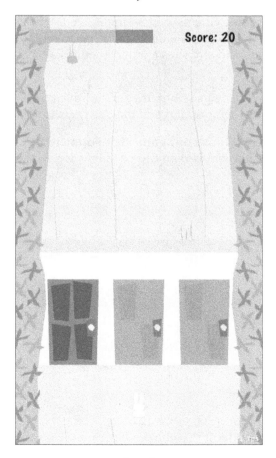

Summary

In this chapter, you learned some advanced techniques that will help you give a professional and complex look to your games.

We started by learning how to create nodes that are composed of several sprites and actions by creating classes that inherit SKNode. In this way, we created a new class for the enemies in the game that consist of two SKSpriteNode instances, two SKAction instances, and the type of enemy.

In addition to this, we learned how we can perform actions on each of the sprites separately so that the element behaves as we want.

Furthermore, I showed you how to apply the parallax effect to our games in order to provide them with depth and a sense of motion. For this purpose, we learned how to take advantage of the update method and combine copies of nodes to run movement actions at different speeds so that it seems that the rabbit is running.

In order to adapt the rabbit to the new movement, we learned how to animate nodes using texture atlases to avoid a decrease in performance. In this way, the main character jumps and smashes against enemies and the wrong doors in a more realistic way.

Finally, we learned how to create geometrical primitives that can be used in several ways in our games by taking advantage of the SKShapeNode class.

In the next chapter, we will finish our game development by applying some elements that will provide a product that is ready to be submitted to the Apple Store.

4
From Basic to Professional Games

In the last chapter, you had a look at how to include some advanced techniques to create games with some complexity. In this chapter, you will incorporate some components in your project, which will complete the game. You will create a condition to end a game and learn how to stop the game and create a *game over* scene. Also, you will add an initial menu to the game and learn how to create transitions between the different scenes of a game. You will also learn how to take advantage of this feature to include a tutorial in the game to teach users how to play it. Finally, you will have an understanding of how to store information, such as the best scores, and load data from external files.

The topics that you will learn in this chapter are as follows:

- How to end a game
- How to add a main menu to the game
- How to create transitions between scenes
- How to develop a tutorial
- How to load and save data

Ending the game

Before going any further, we will need to open the initial project for this chapter, which is similar to the one that we had at the end of the previous chapter. Therefore, unzip 7338_04_Resources.zip, where you will find InsideTheHat_init.zip. Unzip this and open the project with **Xcode**.

We had to look at the code needed to decrease the number of life points as well as the red life bar length. In this section, we will take advantage of this code to end the game when the number of life points is 0.

Usually, when a game is over, everything stops moving and some kind of text alert for the player pops on the screen. So, let's see how we can do this in a SpriteKit project.

For this step, we will need a new label variable. So, let's declare it by adding the following line at the top of GameScene:

```
private var labelGameOver: SKLabelNode!
```

Then, add the following block of code in the resetPositionAction action of the initializeEnemyActions method just after self.updateLifeBar() function:

```
// If we have lost all the life points
if self.lifePoints == 0 {
    self.gameOver()
}
```

When a collision with an enemy happens, we update the life points. If this value equals to 0, we call a new method. So, let's implement it using the following lines:

```
func gameOver() {
    // Initialize the label with a font name
    labelGameOver = SKLabelNode(fontNamed:"MarkerFelt-Thin")
    // Set color, size and position
    labelGameOver.fontColor = UIColor.redColor()
    labelGameOver.fontSize = 60
    labelGameOver.position = CGPoint(x:view!.bounds.size.width/2,
y:view!.bounds.size.height)
    // Specifying zPosition
    labelGameOver.zPosition = 5
    // Set text
    labelGameOver.text = "GAME OVER"
    // Add the label to the scene
    addChild(labelGameOver)
}
```

In this method, we initialized the label variable with the same font as the one that we used for the score label. Then, we set red as its font color and specified a font size that's big enough to cover the screen.

We are going to make the label appear at the top of the screen and in the center using a sequence of actions in order to achieve a dynamic result. This is the reason why we set the label's initial position at the top of the view in the center in a horizontal fashion.

Finally, we specified the zPosition value to ensure that the text is shown over the rest of the elements. We set a piece of text to indicate that the game is over, and we add the label to the scene.

Now that we have the label initialized, it's time to create the movement action that will make it appear dynamically. Add the following block of code at the end of the gameOver method:

```
// Creating movement action
let actionMoveDown = SKAction.moveTo(CGPoint(x:view!.bounds.size.
width/2, y:view!.bounds.size.height/2), duration: 0.25)
// Creating movement action
let actionMoveUp = SKAction.moveTo(CGPoint(x:view!.bounds.size.
width/2, y:view!.bounds.size.height/2 + 60), duration: 0.25)
// Creating block action
let stopGame = SKAction.runBlock {
    // Stop game
    self.view?.paused = true
}
// Creating block action
let stopMusic = SKAction.runBlock {
    // Stop background music
    self.backgroundMusic.stop()
}
```

We created a move action that will bring the label to the center of the screen, and then we created another one that will move it a little upwards.

We also created a runBlock action, where we execute the following command:

```
self.view?.paused = true
```

The paused attribute will set all the animations on the scene to a standby mode and it's a property that we can take advantage of if we want. For example, you can use it to stop the game when the **Configuration** or **Pause** menu is opened.

Finally, we want to stop the background music. Therefore, we created another block action to stop the audio player.

Let's add the last lines at the end of the `gameOver` method:

```
// Creating sequence of actions
let sequence = SKAction.sequence([actionMoveDown, actionMoveUp,
actionMoveDown, stopGame, stopMusic])
// Run sequence
labelGameOver.runAction(sequence)
```

Using the preceding lines, we created a sequence of actions that will combine everything that moves the label from the top of the view to the center: the action that will move it a little upwards and the other action that will recover its position at the center of the view as well as the action that will pause the game and the music.

Finally, on executing this sequence, you will see something that's similar to the following screenshot if you run the game now:

You will realize that the game doesn't stop instantly, because it needs to wait for the **Game Over** label's `move` action to finish before the scene is paused. We can fix it instantly by removing all the actions. But I wanted to show you this `paused` attribute as it can be used in other circumstances.

3-star challenge: restarting a game

We have seen how we can end our game, but what happens if the user wants to play it again? Should they kill the app and restart it just to play a new game? This is not a kind way of treating players. So let's provide them with a way to replay the game easily.

I recommend that you take advantage of all the knowledge that you have acquired so far in order to create a label when the game is over, which will restart the game. With what we have learned in the previous chapters, you will be capable of finding a solution for this challenge.

Try to develop your own solution and then compare it with the following one.

Solution

First of all, we are going to need a label. So let's declare label by adding the following line at the top of GameScene:

```
private var labelResetGame: SKLabelNode!
```

We will initialize labelResetGame when the game is over so that labelResetGame will happen in the gameOver method. For this purpose, replace the following line in the aforementioned method:

```
let sequence = SKAction.sequence([actionMoveDown, actionMoveUp,
actionMoveDown, stopGame, stopMusic])
```

Replace this line with the following lines:

```
// Creating block action
let showLabelResetAction = SKAction.runBlock {
    // Show reset game label
    self.showLabelReset()
}
let sequence = SKAction.sequence([actionMoveDown, actionMoveUp,
actionMoveDown, stopGame, stopMusic, showLabelResetAction])
```

We have created a new `runBlock` action. Therefore, we can make a call to a new method when the game is over. That's the reason why we have added this new action at the end of the sequence. Thus, the new label will be shown just when the game is stopped.

Let's implement this new method by adding the following block of code:

```
func showLabelReset() {
    // Initialize the label with a font name
    labelResetGame = SKLabelNode(fontNamed:"MarkerFelt-Thin")
    // Set color, size and position
    labelResetGame.fontColor = UIColor.greenColor()
    labelResetGame.fontSize = 30
    labelResetGame.position = CGPoint(x:view!.bounds.size.width/2,
y:view!.bounds.size.height/2 - 60)
    // Specifying zPosition
    labelResetGame.zPosition = 5
    // Set text
    labelResetGame.text = "Reset Game"
    // Set node's name
    labelResetGame.name = "reset_label"
    // Add the label to the scene
    addChild(labelResetGame)
}
```

This method will initialize the previously declared `label` with the same font name that we have been using so far. Then, we specified its font color, which will be *green*, and we set its font size and position. Note how we set this label at the center but a little below the initial position.

We want the `label` to be visible. Therefore, we need to specify the `zPosition` value so that it's big enough for the text to be over the rest of the elements in the scene.

Finally, we set its text and specified a key value for its `name` attribute so that we can take advantage of it when identifying whether a user has touched this node. Once the `label` is created, we add it to the scene.

Run the game now, and you will see how this step affects it:

Now, we have to provide this `label` with the functionality of restarting the game. I thought that it would be a good idea to check the `touchesBegan` method to find out whether the user's interactions correspond to the `label`. Therefore, add the following lines at the end of the aforementioned method:

```
// Check if label touched
if self.nodeAtPoint(touch.locationInNode(self)).name == "reset_label"
{
    self.restartGame()
}
```

This means that if the touch location in the scene corresponds to the node named reset_label, we will call a new method. Implement this method using the following block of code:

```
func restartGame() {
    // Reset values
    score = 0
    lastFrameTime = 0
    deltaTime = 0
    // Set doors to nil
    leftDoor = nil
    centerDoor = nil
    rightDoor = nil
    // Remove all children on scene
    self.removeAllChildren()
    // Remove all actions
    self.removeAllActions()
    // Restart the game
    self.view?.presentScene(self)
}
```

When restarting the game, we need to set the initial values of the variables that we use. That's the reason why we set score, lastFrameTime, and deltaTime to 0.

We set the doors variables to nil just to ensure that they are correctly reinitialized. Then, we removed all the children from the scene. So, when the game restarts, everything works fine and there are no errors.

Finally, we removed all the actions in the scene to start the game from scratch and then we called the following method:

```
self.view?.presentScene(self)
```

This will replace the current scene with the specified one, which means that the current scene will replace the specified one with a new instance of the game's scene.

Run the game now, and you will see how we can easily play the game any number of times that we want:

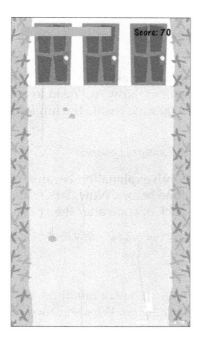

Creating a main menu

When playing mobile games, you will usually find an initial menu screen when you run it. These screens are usually shown to provide players with a way to modify some configurations, such as turning on or turning off of the game sound, the selection of a game's difficulty, or just a way to hide a big load of components.

We are going to create a menu that will be shown when the game is run, where we will show a background and a button to start playing the game.

For this purpose, we will need to create a new scene file to manage this new screen behavior. To do so, perform the following steps:

1. In **Xcode**, select the **File** menu at the top of the screen.

2. Select **New | File**, and you will see the **Files** dialog box.

3. Select the **Swift File** option under **iOS | Source** and click on **Next**.

4. Name it MenuScene and choose the folder where you want it to be saved before clicking on **Create** button.

As you will see, the new file is almost empty. So let's fix this by adding the following lines to the MenuScene.swift file:

```
import SpriteKit
class MenuScene: SKScene {
}
```

We are creating the new file as a subclass of SKScene. Therefore, it will have the potential that the subclass provides. Now, we need to add a background. To do so, add the following variable declaration inside the implementation section of the new class:

```
private var background: SKSpriteNode!
```

This line doesn't need an in-depth explanation because we are just declaring a sprite variable as we have done before. Now, let's initialize it by calling a new method. Add the following block of code after the sprite variable:

```
override func didMoveToView(view: SKView) {
    self.initializeMenu()
}
```

We have added the needed didMoveToView method, and it is mandatory for it to be overridden as a subclass of SKScene. We also called a method, where we will initialize the menu. So let's implement it using the following lines:

```
func initializeMenu() {
    // Initialize menu background
    background = SKSpriteNode(imageNamed: "menu")
    background.zPosition = -1
    background.position = CGPoint(x: (view!.bounds.size.width/2), y:
view!.bounds.size.height/2)
    // Add the background
    addChild(background)
}
```

With these lines of code, we created a new sprite background, specifying a zPosition value, so that it has a position that's lower than that of the view. We set its position so that it is placed at the center of the view and then we added it to the scene.

Before running the game, we need to include some new images for the background. So perform the following steps to achieve this:

1. Right-click on **Art** and select **Add Files to InsideTheHat...**.
2. You'll find `menu.png`, `menu@2x.png`, `menu@2x~ipad.png`, and `menu@3x.png` in the `7338_04_Resources` folder that you unzipped previously. Select these four files and click on **Add**.

At this point, the game will not show the new scene when it is initialized. We first need to make a little change to `GameViewController`. Replace the following line in the `viewDidLoad` method:

```
let scene = GameScene(size: view.bounds.size)
```

Replace this line with the following one:

```
let scene = MenuScene(size: view.bounds.size)
```

In this way, we will initialize the brand new menu as soon as we run the game. So now that everything is ready, execute the project. You will see the following screen:

Now that we have the initial menu, we have no way to play the game. For this purpose, we will need some way to show the game's scene. So keep reading and you will learn how to achieve it.

Transitions and scenes

Usually, games comprise more than one scene. For example, games use a different scene to show a **Configuration** menu, to show the classification table once the game is over, to show a screen with in-app purchases, and so on.

Due to this, we need a way to move between the scenes. The solution that's provided by most game engines is transitions, which are also known as the SKTransition instances in SpriteKit.

The SKTransition class

The SKTransition class inherits from NSObject and provides us with the ability of creating animated transitions between the scenes of the game.

We have several methods in this class that will allow us to create different types of transitions. For example, we can choose one of the following methods:

- crossFadeWithDuration: This method will create a typical cross-faded transition that will take the specified duration to end the transition.

- doorsCloseHorizontalWithDuration: This will create the effect of a door closing horizontally, taking the specified duration to end the door closing event.

- doorsCloseVerticalWithDuration: This will create the effect of a door closing vertically, taking the specified duration to end the door closing event.

- doorsOpenHorizontalWithDuration: This will create the effect of a door opening horizontally, taking the specified duration to end the door closing event.

- doorsOpenVerticalWithDuration: This is similar to the preceding method, but the only difference is that it creates an effect of a door opening vertically.

- doorwayWithDuration: In this case, the outgoing scene disappears as a pair of doors open, while the new scene moves from the background to the foreground.

- fadeWithColor: This transition will first fade to the specified color and then it will fade to the new scene, taking the specified time to finish the process of fading.

- fadeWithDuration: This is similar to the previous one, but in this case, the chosen color is black, and it will take the specified time to finish the fading process but according to the specified time.

- `flipHorizontalWithDuration`: The previous and the next scenes are interchanged by flipping across a horizontal line at the center of the view.

- `flipVerticalWithDuration`: This is similar to the preceding method, but in this case, the previous and the next scenes are interchanged by flipping across a vertical line at the center of the view.

- `moveInWithDirection`: The new scene will appear after following the specified direction (up, down, left, or right), and taking the specified time to finish the process.

- `pushWithDirection`: The new scene appears after following the specified direction (up, down, left, or right), and pushing the previous scene out of view and taking the specified duration to end the scene process.

- `revealWithDirection`: In this case, the scene that moves after following the specified direction is the old one and, while it moves, it will reveal the new scene. This method also allows us to specify a duration value.

- `init(CIFilter:duration)`: This method allows us to create a transition by using a **Core Image** filter and specifying a duration value.

By default, both the outgoing and incoming scenes are paused. Therefore, no actions will happen on any of them, but we can choose to pause just one of them by calling the `pausesIncomingScene` or `pausesOutgoingScene` properties.

Now that we know the different options that we have to make transitions between scenes, let's create one to move from the main menu scene to the game scene.

First of all, we will add a text label in the initial scene that will create the transition when the player touches it. So, let's declare a new variable in `MenuScene`:

```
private var labelInitGame: SKLabelNode!
```

Let's initialize it by adding the following block of code at the end of the `initializeMenu` method:

```
        // Initialize the label with a font name
        labelInitGame = SKLabelNode(fontNamed:"Arial Bold")
        // Set color, size and position
        labelInitGame.fontColor = UIColor(red: 0.929, green: 0.129,
blue: 0.486, alpha: 1.0)
        labelInitGame.fontSize = 60
        labelInitGame.position = CGPoint(x:view!.bounds.size.width/2,
y:view!.bounds.size.height/2)
        // Set text
        labelInitGame.text = "Init Game"
```

```
// Set node's name
labelInitGame.name = "init_game_label"

// Add the label to the scene
addChild(labelInitGame)
```

We initialized the `label` in a way that's similar to how we have initialized labels previously. We first created the label by specifying a font name. Then, we set its position. This time, we wanted to set the `label` with the same color as that of the rabbit's snout. Therefore, we created the `UIColor` object with the `red`, `green`, and `blue` attributes.

 In order to specify the `red`, `green`, and `blue` attributes values, you need to choose the `CGFloat` values between `0.0` and `1.0`.

We also set the `alpha` property to `1.0` value because we want the `label` to be fully visible. Then, we specified the font size and set `label` at the center of the view.

As we want the `label` to show its purpose, we set its text and specified the node's name property so that it can be used later to check whether screen has been touched.

Finally, we added it to the scene. Now, run the game and have a look at the results:

Now that we have the label on the screen, we just need to add its functionality. You can detect when it has been touched by adding the following lines of code:

```
override func touchesBegan(touches: Set<UITouch>, withEvent event:
UIEvent?) {
    if let touch = touches.first {
        let location = touch.locationInNode(self)
        // Check if label touched
        if self.nodeAtPoint(location).name == "init_game_label" {
            self.initGame()
        }
    }
}
```

We have overridden the `touchesBegan` method so that we can detect and handle the touches on this scene. In this method, we take the location of the first touch and check whether the touch coincides with the `init` game label.

If it does, we call a new method, which can be implemented with the following block of code:

```
func initGame() {
    // Create scene transition
    let sceneTransition = SKTransition.
doorsOpenVerticalWithDuration(1.25)
    // Create next scene
    let gameScene = GameScene(size: view!.bounds.size)
    // Present next scene with transition
    self.view?.presentScene(gameScene, transition: sceneTransition)
}
```

We first created a scene transition that will show the next scene while the first menu disappears vertically, taking `1.25` seconds for the transition.

Then, we created the next scene that we want to show, which was created using the view's size as usual. Finally, we presented the new scene using the desired transition.

Run the game now and have a look at the new transition, but you can choose the one that you prefer:

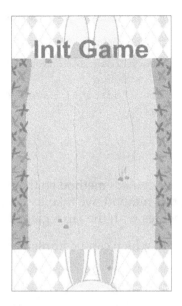

Creating a tutorial

When we first play a game, we usually go through a guided path called a tutorial that will show us how to play the game. This path will just let us perform some specific actions so that the players learn the mechanics of the game and the operations that are allowed in the game.

The best way of developing a tutorial is by thinking about it as a state machine, where each state corresponds to one step of the tutorial and where we can specify the actions allowed on each state and learn how to pass from one state to the next one.

In this section, we are going to develop a tutorial that will consist of five states or steps, where some visual elements will teach players how to implement them.

For this purpose, we will need to create an enumerated object to handle the different steps of the tutorial. So add the following lines at the top of the GameScene class just after the import section:

```
enum TutorialSteps : UInt32 {
    case TUTORIAL_STEP_1 = 0
    case TUTORIAL_STEP_2 = 1
    case TUTORIAL_STEP_3 = 2
```

```
        case TUTORIAL_STEP_4 = 3
        case TUTORIAL_STEP_5 = 4
        case TUTORIAL_ENDED = 5
}
```

As you can see, the enumeration consists of five tutorial steps and a step to specify that the tutorial has finished.

As we want to show some visual elements so that players understand how to play the game, we will need some variables. So add the following block of code just after `private var labelResetGame: SKLabelNode!`:

```
    private var tutorialStep: TutorialSteps = .TUTORIAL_STEP_1
    private var tutorialImage: SKSpriteNode!
    private var labelTutorial: SKLabelNode!
    private var tutorialFrame: SKShapeNode!
```

We initialized one variable to store the tutorial steps that will allow us to know which information needs to be shown each time (this is initialized to the first step), a sprite to show an image of a hand, and a label that shows an explanatory text. We also declared a shape node, as we are going to take advantage of it to frame the different places where players can touch.

To initialize the tutorial, we are going to perform a call to a new method. So, add the following lines at the beginning of `didMoveToView`:

```
    // If it's the first time the tutorial appears
    if tutorialStep != .TUTORIAL_ENDED {
        self.initializeTutorial()
    }
```

If the tutorial step is not the last one, which means that the tutorial has finished successfully, we will initialize it by calling the following method:

```
func initializeTutorial() {
    // Create action
    let pauseForTutorial = SKAction.runBlock {
        // Pause game for the tutorial
        self.view?.paused = true
        // Initialize tutorial image
        self.tutorialImage = SKSpriteNode(imageNamed: "hand")
        // Set image position
        self.tutorialImage.position = CGPoint(x:self.view!.bounds.
size.width/6, y: self.view!.bounds.size.height/3)
```

```
        // Specifying zPosition
        self.tutorialImage.zPosition = 7
        // Add the image to the scene
        self.addChild(self.tutorialImage)
    }
}
```

We'll take advantage of this method to initialize the different elements that will help us guide the player. We will stop the game and show the first state of the tutorial. This is the reason why we are going to initialize the variables in a `runBlock` action.

In this block, we pause the game and initialize the hand node, setting it in the middle of the first third of the screen. We specify its `zPosition` value, as we want it to be fully visible. Then, we add it to the scene.

Now, add the following block of code at the end of `pauseForTutorial`:

```
// Initialize tutorial frame
self.tutorialFrame = SKShapeNode(rectOfSize: CGSize(width: self.view!.
bounds.width/3, height: self.view!.bounds.size.height))
// Set frame's position
self.tutorialFrame.position = CGPoint(x:self.view!.bounds.size.
width/6, y: self.view!.bounds.size.height/2)
// No border
self.tutorialFrame.lineWidth = 0
// Specify zPosition
self.tutorialFrame.zPosition = 6
// Set frame color
self.tutorialFrame.fillColor = UIColor.whiteColor()
// Set alpha value
self.tutorialFrame.alpha = 0.5
// Set node's name
self.tutorialFrame.name = "tutorial_frame"
// Add frame to scene
self.addChild(self.tutorialFrame)
```

We initialized the frame so that it will cover the first third of the view (the one on the left), from the top to the bottom, specifying that we don't want it to have borders, and we set its `zPosition` property in such a way that it is above the image of the hand.

Then, we specified its color and `alpha` values so that we can see it as a highlighted zone, and we specified a name value to use it as an identifier for touches. Finally, we added the frame to the scene.

We still need to initialize the `label`. So, add the following lines of code at the end of `pauseForTutorial`:

```
// Initialize label
self.labelTutorial = SKLabelNode(fontNamed:"MarkerFelt-Thin")
// Set color, size and position
self.labelTutorial.fontColor = UIColor.blackColor()
self.labelTutorial.fontSize = 30
self.labelTutorial.position.x = self.tutorialImage.position.x
self.labelTutorial.position.y = self.tutorialImage.position.y + 50
// Specifying zPosition
self.labelTutorial.zPosition = 7
// Set text
self.labelTutorial.text = "Touch"
// Add the label to the scene
self.addChild(self.labelTutorial)
```

With these lines, we initialized the `label` the way we are used to doing by specifying the same font and color used in the score label. We chose a size that's large enough to make the `label` clearly visible, and we set it on the left-hand side of the screen, a little above the hand node. Then, we set its `zPosition` property and text and added it to the scene.

Once we have the tutorial elements on the screen, we just need to show them. So, add the following block at the end of `initializeTutorial`:

```
// Creating a delay action
let delayAction = SKAction.waitForDuration(1.0)
let sequence = SKAction.sequence([delayAction, pauseForTutorial])
// Running the non-ending sequence
self.runAction(sequence)
```

We created a `delay` action so that the tutorial will be shown one second after the game is initialized, and then we showed the information of the first state of the tutorial.

Execute the project now, and you will see how it looks:

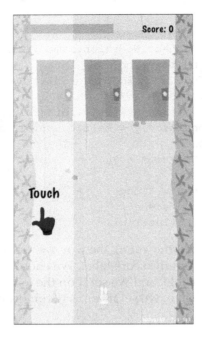

Updating the tutorial steps

As you can see, the game is paused, and it should start when we touch the frame to the left. So, let's add the needed code for this purpose.

Replace the following line in `touchesBegan`:

```
self.moveRabbitToNextLocation(location)
```

Replace the preceding line with the following block of code:

```
if self.tutorialStep != .TUTORIAL_ENDED && self.nodeAtPoint(location).
name == "tutorial_frame" {
    self.updateTutorial()
} else if self.tutorialStep == .TUTORIAL_ENDED {
    self.moveRabbitToNextLocation(location)
}
```

With the preceding block of code, we specified that we want to update the tutorial step if the tutorial is being shown and we have touched the frame. In this way, the game will remain paused. If the condition doesn't match and we are sure that the tutorial has ended, we move the rabbit where the player has touched. Thus, we handle the game when the tutorial is finished.

Let's implement this new `updateTutorial` method. Add the following block of code in `updateTutorial()` method:

```
func updateTutorial() {
    // Auxiliar variables
    var moveAction:SKAction!
    var duration: CGFloat = 0.0
    var nextPosition: CGPoint
    switch tutorialStep {
        default: break
    }
}
```

We are just adding the skeleton of the method in which we create some auxiliary variables that will help us update the tutorial steps. We also added a `switch` statement, where we will add the different tutorial steps to manage what will happen in each step.

Let's start with the first one. Add the following block of code just above `default: break`:

```
case .TUTORIAL_STEP_1:
    // Hide tutorial elements
    self.tutorialImage.hidden = true
    self.labelTutorial.hidden = true
    self.tutorialFrame.hidden = true
    // Setting the next position
    nextPosition = CGPoint(x: leftDoor.position.x, y: rabbit.
position.y)
    // We want the rabbit to move on a constant speed
    duration = self.distanceBetween(point: self.rabbit.position,
andPoint: nextPosition) / 360.0
    // Move the rabbit to the touched position
    moveAction = SKAction.moveToX(nextPosition.x, duration:
Double(duration))
```

```
    let updateTutorialAction = SKAction.runBlock {
        // Update tutorial step
        self.tutorialStep = .TUTORIAL_STEP_2
        self.updateTutorial()
    }
    // Create sequence
    let sequence = SKAction.sequence([moveAction,updateTutorialActi
on])
    // Run the sequence
    self.rabbit.runAction(sequence)
    // Release the game for the tutorial
    self.view?.paused = false
break
```

This case will be reached when we run the first state and the player touches on the tutorial frame. At this point, we will hide all the visual elements and move the rabbit to the center of the left door.

For this purpose, we specified the next position and the duration to reach the next position, and we created a movement action with this information.

Then, we created a `runBlock` action where we updated the tutorial step and called the `updateTutorial` method again.

Finally, we created a sequence with both the actions and we released the game so that this results in a situation where, once the player touches on the left frame, the tutorial element will disappear, the game will continue, and it will execute the code in the second step after a delay.

Let's implement this second step by adding the following code one step before `default: break`:

```
    case .TUTORIAL_STEP_2:
        // Create action
        let pauseForTutorial = SKAction.runBlock {
            // Pause game for the tutorial
            self.view?.paused = true
            // Update tutorial image
            self.tutorialImage.position = CGPoint(x:5*self.view!.bounds.
size.width/6, y: self.view!.bounds.size.height/3)
            self.tutorialImage.hidden = false

            // Update tutorial frame
            self.tutorialFrame.position = CGPoint(x:5*self.view!.bounds.
size.width/6, y: self.view!.bounds.size.height/2)
            self.tutorialFrame.hidden = false
```

```
            // Update tutorial label
            self.labelTutorial.position.x = self.tutorialImage.position.x
            self.labelTutorial.hidden = false
            // Update tutorial step
            self.tutorialStep = .TUTORIAL_STEP_3
        }
        // Creating a delay action
        let delayAction = SKAction.waitForDuration(4.25)
        // Create sequence
        let sequence = SKAction.sequence([delayAction, pauseForTutorial])
        // Run the sequence
        self.runAction(sequence)
    break
```

In this step, we executed a block where we first pause the game and then show the same tutorial information as that in the first step, but on the right-hand side this time. We also updated the `tutorialStep` variable so that the tutorial progresses.

We want the preceding code to be triggered after a delay, which is why we created a delay action and run it in a sequence.

If you run the game now, you will see what's shown in the following screenshot:

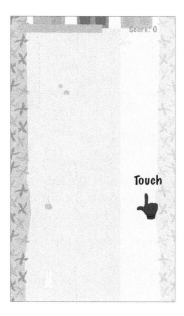

Now, we want the game to react when we touch on the right-hand side of the screen while the tutorial is being shown. So, let's implement the third state with the following lines:

```
case .TUTORIAL_STEP_3:
    // Hide tutorial elements
    self.tutorialImage.hidden = true
    self.labelTutorial.hidden = true
    self.tutorialFrame.hidden = true
    // Release the game for the tutorial
    self.view?.paused = false
    // Setting the next position
    nextPosition = CGPoint(x: rightDoor.position.x, y: rabbit.
position.y)
    // We want the rabbit to move on a constant speed
    duration = self.distanceBetween(point: self.rabbit.position,
andPoint: nextPosition) / 360.0
    // Move the rabbit to the touched position
    moveAction = SKAction.moveToX(nextPosition.x, duration:
Double(duration))
    // Create action
    let updateTutorialAction = SKAction.runBlock {
        // Update tutorial step
        self.tutorialStep = .TUTORIAL_STEP_4
        self.updateTutorial()
    }
    // Create sequence
    let sequence = SKAction.sequence([moveAction,
updateTutorialAction])
    // Run the sequence
    self.rabbit.runAction(sequence)
break
```

This step is similar to the first one; we hide the tutorial elements and then release the game while we move the rabbit to the right of the screen, centered at the door, thanks to a movement action.

We created a `runBlock` action to update the tutorial step and call the `updateTutorial` method again.

Finally, we created a sequence with both the actions and ran it. At this point, we need to implement the fourth state of the tutorial to continue. So, let's add the following block of code:

```
case .TUTORIAL_STEP_4:
    // Create action
    let pauseForTutorial = SKAction.runBlock {
        // Set image position
        self.tutorialImage.position = CGPoint(x:self.view!.bounds.
size.width/2, y: self.view!.bounds.size.height/3)
        // Update tutorial label
        self.labelTutorial.text = "RUN!"
        self.labelTutorial.position.x = self.tutorialImage.position.x
        self.labelTutorial.hidden = false
        // Update tutorial step
        self.tutorialStep = .TUTORIAL_STEP_5
        self.updateTutorial()
    }
    // Creating a delay action
    let delayAction = SKAction.waitForDuration(2.25)
    // Create sequence
    let sequence = SKAction.sequence([delayAction, pauseForTutorial])
    // Run the sequence
    self.runAction(sequence)
break
```

When we reach this state, we will pause the game again after a delay. When the game is paused again, we move the `text` label to the center of the screen, change its text, and then show it. We also update the tutorial step to the next one.

In the preceding code, we also created a `delay` action and ran a `sequence` with both the actions. So, if we run the game now, we will see something that's similar to what's shown in the following screenshot:

Now, let's see what will happen in the last step of the tutorial. Add the following lines just before `default:` `break`:

```
case .TUTORIAL_STEP_5:
    // Create action
    let endOfMovementAction = SKAction.runBlock {
        // Remove tutorial elements
        self.tutorialImage.removeFromParent()
        self.labelTutorial.removeFromParent()
        self.tutorialFrame.removeFromParent()
        // Update tutorial step
        self.tutorialStep = .TUTORIAL_ENDED
    }
```

```
    // Creating a delay action
    let delayAction = SKAction.waitForDuration(1.25)
    // Create sequence
    let sequence = SKAction.sequence([delayAction,endOfMovementActi
on])
    // Run the sequence
    self.runAction(sequence)
break
```

When we arrive at this point, we create an action where we will remove the visual elements from the view and update the tutorial step to the last one so that the game code understands that the game can continue without interruptions.

We want to execute it after a delay. Therefore, the last text is shown for a few seconds. This is the reason why we build a sequence with the aforementioned `runBlock` object and a `delay` action.

Run the game again and play it. You will see how we can play as much as we want by restarting the game, but we will see the tutorial only once:

If you develop a tutorial for another game, it will be completely different from this one, but I recommend that you break down all the concepts that you want to learn in several states so that you can ensure that the player has complete knowledge to build and start playing the game.

Loading and saving data

When playing games, users will usually need a way to store how far they have arrived in the game or some other information, such as the best score or the main character's name. Due to this, the game will be able to load this stored data or some other data, such as the position of the enemies in each level of the game.

In this section, we are going to learn how to store the maximum score that a player has reached so far. For this purpose, we are going to take advantage of the NSUserDefaults class.

The NSUserDefaults class

This class provides an interface to read and write information on the default system. This default system is the place where the preferences that are chosen on your game or app, such as the user's language, sound (enabled or disabled), and so on, will be stored.

A user default values can be of different types, such as Boolean, float, integer, double, string, data, array, and so on, and the NSUserDefaults class provides methods for all of them.

We are going to use NSUserDefaults class to store the best score achieved by the player. So for this purpose, we will need some new variables. Add them to the top of GameScene, as follows:

```
private var labelBestScore: SKLabelNode!
private var bestScore: Int = 0
private var userDefaults: NSUserDefaults!
private var kUserDefaultBestScore = "user_default_best_score"
```

We declared a new label that will show the best score, which will be kept by a new integer variable. We also declared an instance of NSUserDefaults and a constant that will help us identify the user's default name.

The next step is to initialize the user defaults. Add the following method call at the beginning of didMoveToView:

```
self.initializeUserDefaults()
```

Initialize this method using the following block of code:

```
func initializeUserDefaults() {
    // Initialize user defaults
    if (userDefaults == nil) {
        userDefaults = NSUserDefaults.standardUserDefaults()
    }
    // If the user default exists
    if userDefaults.integerForKey(kUserDefaultBestScore) > 0 {
        bestScore = userDefaults.integerForKey(kUserDefaultBestScore)
    }
}
```

We first initialized the user's `default` variables, if it is null, and then we got the value of the stored best score, if it has been previously updated. We performed this last action so that every time we execute the game it will show the correct value.

> We used the `integerForKey` method as we expect to store integer values in this user's `default` variable.

If the user's `default` exists, we update the `bestScore` value so that it can be used later.

The next step is to create a new `label`. Let's add some code to the `initializeLabels` variable and add the following lines of code at the end of the aforementioned method:

```
// Initialize the label as a copy
labelBestScore = labelScore.copy() as! SKLabelNode
// Set color, size and position
labelBestScore.fontColor = UIColor.orangeColor()
labelBestScore.position.y = labelScore.position.y - 30
// Set text
labelBestScore.text = "Best: \(bestScore)"
// Add the label to the scene
addChild(labelBestScore)
```

We initialized this label as a copy of the previous one so that we can reuse some of its properties. We just want it to have a different color. Therefore, we chose the orange one and placed it below the score label.

Then we set its text, which is composed by a string, and the value of the best score variable, and finally we added it to the scene.

If you run the game now, you will see this new `label` at the top right of the screen, as shown in the following screenshot:

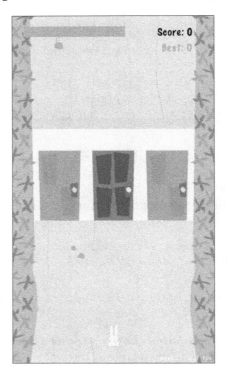

Now that we have the `label` in the view that will get the information stored in the user's `default` values, we just need to update its user's `default` values where applicable.

The perfect moment to update it is when the game is over. Let's add the following line to `gameOver` just after `addChild(labelGameOver)`:

```
// Update best score
self.updateBestScore()
```

This will call a new method that we need to implement using the following lines:

```
func updateBestScore() {
    if score > bestScore {
        userDefaults.setInteger(score, forKey: kUserDefaultBestScore)
        labelBestScore.text = "Best: \(score)"
    }
}
```

In this method, we first checked whether the new score that was accomplished is greater than the best one, and if this is the case, we set this new value to the user's `default` value that is specified by the constant that we declared previously. Then, we updated the `label` too.

 You have to specify the same user's `default` value that's used when you are storing as the one that's used when we are loading the data.

Run the game now and see what happens when the game finishes:

If you kill the game process and start playing again, you will see how the best score value is updated correctly. However, everything will be deleted if you remove the game from your device.

2-star challenge: completing the tutorial

You may have realized that the tutorial reappears every time we rerun the game even if it has been completed previously. Now that we know how to store information on the device, let's take advantage of it in order to store information about whether the tutorial has been completed.

Solution

We will need a couple of new variables to support this new behavior. Therefore, add the following lines at the top of `GameScene` class:

```
private var isTutorialCompleted: Bool = false
private var kUserDefaultTutorialCompleted = "user_default_tutorial_
completed"
```

We declared a Boolean variable that will act as a `flag` that represents the user's `default` value. We also declared a constant that will be used to identify the value of the desired user default.

This new flag will be initialized in `initializeUserDefaults`. So add the following block of code at the end of the aforementioned method:

```
if userDefaults.boolForKey(kUserDefaultTutorialCompleted) {
    isTutorialCompleted = userDefaults.boolForKey(kUserDefaultTutoria
lCompleted)
}
```

The preceding code will get the value stored in the user's `default` in case value already exists. If this is not the case, it will keep the value that was set by user's `default` when initialized (`false`).

Now, we need to update the user's `default` value, and this will happen at the end of the fifth step of the tutorial. So, go to `case .TUTORIAL_STEP_5` of `updateTutorial` and add the following lines just after `self.tutorialStep = .TUTORIAL_ENDED`:

```
// Update tutorial flag
self.isTutorialCompleted = true
self.userDefaults.setBool(self.isTutorialCompleted, forKey: self.
kUserDefaultTutorialCompleted)
```

When the tutorial reaches the last step, we update the `flag` and the user's `default`.

Finally, we just need to take advantage of this new `flag` to know when to show the tutorial. Let's make a couple of changes. In `didMoveToView`, replace the following line:

```
if tutorialStep != .TUTORIAL_ENDED {
```

Replace the preceding line of code with the following:

```
if !isTutorialCompleted && tutorialStep != .TUTORIAL_ENDED {
```

In this way, when trying to initialize the tutorial, we will also take into account the new flag.

The last change that we need to perform is in `touchesBegan`, where we check whether the tutorial has ended. Hence, replace the following lines:

```
if self.tutorialStep != .TUTORIAL_ENDED && self.nodeAtPoint(location).
name == "tutorial_frame" {
    self.updateTutorial()
} else if self.tutorialStep == .TUTORIAL_ENDED {
    self.moveRabbitToNextLocation(location)
}
```

Replace the preceding block of code with the following lines:

```
if !isTutorialCompleted && self.tutorialStep != .TUTORIAL_ENDED &&
self.nodeAtPoint(location).name == "tutorial_frame" {
    self.updateTutorial()
} else if isTutorialCompleted || self.tutorialStep == .TUTORIAL_ENDED
    {
        self.moveRabbitToNextLocation(location)
    }
```

In both the cases, we just add the new flag as a condition and everything will work smoothly now. So, execute the project and check out this new behavior:

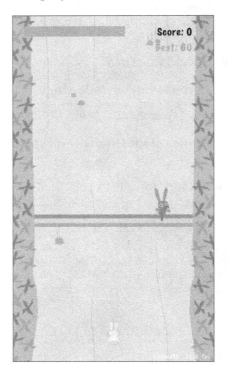

The property list files

Apart from the loading of data from user's `default`, there is a more powerful way to get information from an external source. It's called the **known property files**, which are also known as the `plist` files.

These files are very common in iOS development. For example, they are used to store the configuration values of projects in `Info.plist`.

The property list files contain a list of keys that can contain different types of values, such as dictionaries, strings, numbers, dates, or Boolean values and we are going to take advantage of them to store the information of each door for all the waves that we want to load.

This approach is the one that you will use if you create a game with several levels, and each level has some specific information that you want to load once you initialize the new scene.

In our case, we are going to simulate that we are loading the information of level 1 of the game from a `plist` file. From this file, we will get the number of waves that the level has and the distribution of the correct and wrong doors in each wave.

First of all, let's add the corresponding file to the project by performing the following steps:

1. Right-click on **Art** and select **Add Files to InsideTheHat...**.

2. You'll find `Level_info.plist` in the `7338_04_Resources` folder that you previously unzipped. Select this file and click on **Add**.

You will see something that's similar to what's shown in the following screenshot:

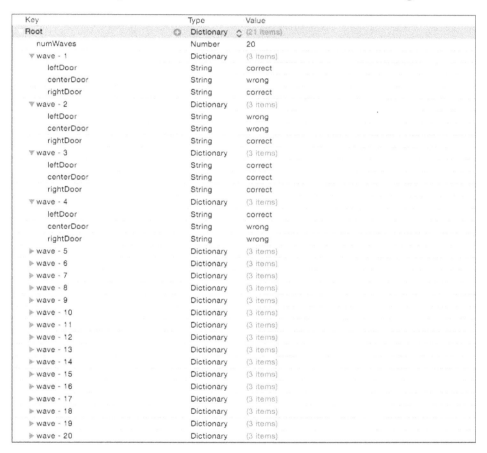

Key	Type	Value
Root	Dictionary	(21 items)
numWaves	Number	20
▼ wave - 1	Dictionary	(3 items)
leftDoor	String	correct
centerDoor	String	wrong
rightDoor	String	correct
▼ wave - 2	Dictionary	(3 items)
leftDoor	String	wrong
centerDoor	String	wrong
rightDoor	String	correct
▼ wave - 3	Dictionary	(3 items)
leftDoor	String	correct
centerDoor	String	correct
rightDoor	String	correct
▼ wave - 4	Dictionary	(3 items)
leftDoor	String	correct
centerDoor	String	wrong
rightDoor	String	wrong
▶ wave - 5	Dictionary	(3 items)
▶ wave - 6	Dictionary	(3 items)
▶ wave - 7	Dictionary	(3 items)
▶ wave - 8	Dictionary	(3 items)
▶ wave - 9	Dictionary	(3 items)
▶ wave - 10	Dictionary	(3 items)
▶ wave - 11	Dictionary	(3 items)
▶ wave - 12	Dictionary	(3 items)
▶ wave - 13	Dictionary	(3 items)
▶ wave - 14	Dictionary	(3 items)
▶ wave - 15	Dictionary	(3 items)
▶ wave - 16	Dictionary	(3 items)
▶ wave - 17	Dictionary	(3 items)
▶ wave - 18	Dictionary	(3 items)
▶ wave - 19	Dictionary	(3 items)
▶ wave - 20	Dictionary	(3 items)

Note that you can create your own `plist` file using the **iOS** | **Resource** | **Property List** option in the **New File** menu.

As you can see in the preceding screenshot, this file contains a key called `numWaves` that contains the number of waves of the first level (`20`) and a list of dictionaries that contains three strings for each wave. Each of these strings corresponds to one of the doors in a wave, and its value can be `correct` or `wrong`, depending on how we want the wave to be loaded.

Now that we know how information is distributed in a property list file, it's time to read it. So, let's declare some variables that we will need for this purpose:

```
private var maxWaves: Int = 0
private var waveNumber: Int = 1
private var leftDoorsInfo: [String]!
private var centerDoorsInfo: [String]!
private var rightDoorsInfo: [String]!
```

We declared a variable to store the maximum number of waves that were read from the file and a variable that will keep the count of waves loaded.

We also declared three arrays of strings that will be used to store information of each wave for each door.

Now, let's initialize the level information. Add the following method call at the beginning of `didMoveToView`:

```
self.readLevelInfo()
```

Implement it using the following block of code:

```
self.readLevelInfo()
//Implement it using the following block of code:
func readLevelInfo() {
    // Declare dictionary variable
    var levelDictionary: NSDictionary!
    var waveInfo: NSDictionary
    leftDoorsInfo = [String]()
    centerDoorsInfo = [String]()
    rightDoorsInfo = [String]()
    // Get level dictionary root
    if let path = NSBundle.mainBundle().pathForResource("Level_info",
ofType: "plist") {
        levelDictionary = NSDictionary(contentsOfFile: path)
    }
```

```
    // Initialize max number of waves
    maxWaves = levelDictionary!.valueForKey("numWaves") as! Int
    // Get info for all the waves
    for var i: Int = 1; i <= maxWaves; i++ {
        waveInfo = levelDictionary!.valueForKey("wave - \(i)") as!
NSDictionary
      leftDoorsInfo.append(waveInfo.valueForKey("leftDoor") as! String)
        centerDoorsInfo.append(waveInfo.valueForKey("centerDoor")as!
String)
        rightDoorsInfo.append(waveInfo.valueForKey("rightDoor")as!
String)
    }
}
```

We first initialized two NSDictionary variables. The first one will be used to store the whole dictionary, and the second one will get information of each wave's dictionary. Then, we initialized the arrays so that they can begin storing values.

To get the dictionary's root, we need to get the file's path using the pathForResource method, specifying the filename and its extension. Once we have the path, we can initialize the dictionary with the contents of the file.

Then, we get the numWaves value from the file thanks to the valueForKey method, where we specify the desired key and force its type to be an integer.

We created a for loop, where we will find the information of each wave by getting each waveInfo dictionary and distributing the left, center, and right door values to the corresponding array.

Now that we have loaded the information, it's time to use it to create a level. Let's make a couple of changes to setDoorAttributes. Replace the following line of code of each case:

```
if (arc4random_uniform(2) == 0) {
```

Replace the preceding line of code with the corresponding lines from the following code:

```
if leftDoorsInfo[waveNumber-1] == "wrong" {
if centerDoorsInfo[waveNumber-1] == "wrong" {
if rightDoorsInfo[waveNumber-1] == "wrong" {
```

In this way, we created the doors, depending on the already loaded information. Finally, we need to update the wave count. Add the following lines at the end of `initializeWave`:

```
// Increase wave
if waveNumber < maxWaves {
    waveNumber++
} else {
    waveNumber = 1
}
```

We increase the counter if we haven't reached the maximum value. In such a situation, we reset it to 1. Thus, the game will create an endless loop, but you can change it for things such as a **Game Over** call.

Finally, we need to reset this value when the game is restarted. Add the following line at the beginning of `restartGame`:

```
waveNumber = 1
```

Run the game now, and you will see how the game now loads the doors as we specified in the `property list` file:

Summary

This chapter helped you learn how to add some essential elements that will transform the game into a complete product that's ready to be uploaded to the App Store.

We began by using the **Game Over** condition to finish the game. We also added a way to restart the game the number of times that we want. Then, we added a main menu scene that helped us learn how to create transitions between the scenes of the game. We used this new scene to see how a tutorial should be created as a states machine, and we created a tutorial for the game so that the players know the mechanics of the game as soon as they play the game for the first time. Finally, we learned how to load and save data of the game by using the user's `default` values or `property list` files.

In the next chapter, we will take advantage of the iOS devices to learn some available techniques.

5
Utilizing the Hardware and Graphics Processor

In the last chapter, we learned some techniques that helped us give our game an aspect of a complete and marketable product. In the following pages, we will make use of the capabilities of mobile devices as well as the accelerometer to add dynamic behavior. We will also learn some visual techniques, the use of **shaders**, and ways to add lighting and shadows to a game.

You will learn the following things in this chapter:

- How to use the accelerometer
- How to add shaders to the game
- How to add lighting and shadows to the game

Using the accelerometer

One of the best technological advances brought by mobile devices is the accelerometer, which is a hardware mechanism that provides the capability of measuring the G-force acceleration on the x, y, and z coordinates.

This technology opened a wide field of new types of games and helped modernize some existing genres. We are going to utilize it to provide a new way to control the rabbit's movement.

In order to start receiving information from the accelerometer, we are going to import a new framework to our project. But first of all, let's open the initial project for this chapter, which is similar to the one that we left at the end of the previous chapter, by performing the following steps:

1. Unzip 7338_05_Resources.zip, where you will find InsideTheHat_init.zip. Unzip it too and open the project with **Xcode**.

2. If you take a look to its contents, you will see that we are not using the plist file information anymore to load the door's distribution.

Now that we have the basis of the development, add the following import statement at the top of GameScene:

```
import CoreMotion
```

This iOS framework will give our game the ability to receive and process motion data from an iPhone's or iPad's hardware.

The CoreMotion framework provides several classes such as CMAltimeter, CMAttitude, CMPedometer, and CMSensorRecorder to control and process different types of motion data, but we will focus on CMMotionManager for our game.

The CMMotionManager class

The CMMotionManager class provides information such as the rotation rate, accelerometer data, altitude, and magnetometer data, which are generated by the accelerometer, magnetometer, and gyroscope mechanisms that are available on every device.

We are going to center ourselves on the accelerometer data that is provided by the CMAccelerometerData class and the methods that it provides.

Let's start by declaring some variables that we will use during this development. Add the following lines after private var rightDoorsInfo: [String]!:

```
private var motionManager: CMMotionManager!
private var accelerometerData: CMAccelerometerData!
private var acceleration: CMAcceleration!
```

We declared the CMMotionManager, CMAccelerometerData, and CMAcceleration instances, which are the objects that are needed to manage the accelerometer-related information.

To initialize these objects, add the following line at the beginning of didMoveToView:

```
self.initializeAccelerometer()
```

Implement it using the following block of code:

```
func initializeAccelerometer() {
    // Initialize motion manager
    self.motionManager = CMMotionManager()

    // Start receiving accelerometer data
    self.motionManager.startAccelerometerUpdates()
}
```

In the previous code, we just initialized the `motion` manager and called the `startAccelerometerUpdates` function that is responsible for receiving the accelerometer-related information.

 We just need to create a `motion` manager instance as, thanks to it, we can retrieve all the `motion` data that we need.

We are going to continuously check the accelerometer-related information. The best place to do this is in the `update` method. So, add the following method call at the end of this method:

```
// Get accelerometer data
self.useAccelerometerData()
```

Implement the preceding lines of code using the following lines of code:

```
func useAccelerometerData() {
    if self.motionManager != nil {
        // Getting accelerometer data
        self.accelerometerData = self.motionManager.accelerometerData

        // Getting acceleration
        self.acceleration = self.accelerometerData.acceleration

        // Calculate next position on X coordinate
        var nextPositionX: CGFloat = self.rabbit.position.x +
CGFloat(acceleration.x) * 1500.0 * CGFloat(deltaTime)

        // Keep the rabbit inside bounds
        if nextPositionX + self.rabbit.size.width/2 >
        self.rightDoor.position.x + self.rightDoor.size.width/2
        {
            nextPositionX = self.rightDoor.position.x +
self.rightDoor.size.width/2 - self.rabbit.size.width/2
        }
        else if nextPositionX - self.rabbit.size.width/2 <
        self.leftDoor.position.x - self.leftDoor.size.width/2 {
```

```
          nextPositionX = self.leftDoor.position.x -
    self.leftDoor.size.width/2 + self.rabbit.size.width/2
        }
          // Set new position
          self.rabbit.position.x = nextPositionX
      }
  }
```

If the `motion` manager is ready, we obtain its accelerometer data and update the `accelerometerData` variable with this information.

Then, we get the `acceleration` data from the accelerometer and calculate the next position on the *x* coordinate. We calculate it by multiplying a constant (`1500.0`) by the `delta` time that we updated in the `updateParallaxLayers` method and by the acceleration on the *x* coordinate.

 I've specified a value of `1500.0` as it's convenient to create a movement that's fast enough for the game, but you can change this value according to your requirements.

Once the next position is calculated, we just want it to be kept inside the bounds of our game. That's the reason why we specify the maximum and minimum values that the rabbit can take on the *x* coordinate. Finally, we set the rabbit's new position to `sprite`.

When the game is over, we should stop reading the accelerometer information as it is no longer needed until the game is restarted. So, add the following line to the `gameOver` method at the beginning of the `stopGame` block:

```
// Stop receiving accelerometer data
self.motionManager.stopAccelerometerUpdates()
```

In this way, `self.motionManager.stopAccelerometerUpdates()` will stop receiving data from the accelerometer, and we will start receiving it again when a user restarts the game.

We just need to remove the block of code corresponding to the `touchesBegan` method that corresponds to the rabbit's movement. So, delete the following lines from this method, as they will not be needed anymore:

```
if isMovementAllowed {
    // Moving the rabbit to the touched position
    let location = touch.locationInNode(self)
    if !isTutorialCompleted && self.tutorialStep !=
.TUTORIAL_ENDED && self.nodeAtPoint(location).name ==
"tutorial_frame" {
        self.updateTutorial()
```

```
        } else if isTutorialCompleted || self.tutorialStep ==
.TUTORIAL_ENDED {
            self.moveRabbitToNextLocation(location)
        }
    }
```

Also, remove the call to the tutorial from `didMoveToView`:

```
// If it's the first time the tutorial appears
if !isTutorialCompleted && tutorialStep != .TUTORIAL_ENDED {
    self.initializeTutorial()
}
```

Okay, now that everything is ready, we can check out what we have developed so far. Run the game on a physical device and look at the new behavior!

 You can only test the accelerometer on physical devices as the Xcode's simulator doesn't provide this capability.

If you run the game now, you will see what's shown in the following screenshot:

Don't worry if the rabbit can now strangely pass through the wall; we want just to learn how to handle the accelerometer data.

It's possible that you haven't realized that this code has some weaknesses, because it's quite probable that you are standing and your device is almost vertically and horizontally leveled. But what will happen if you want to play while lying on one side or you want to use the *y* coordinate acceleration too?

Let's add a couple of lines to check this. So copy and paste the following lines to `useAccelerometerData` after creating the `nextPositionX` object:

```
print("acceleration on X: \(CGFloat(acceleration.x))")
print("acceleration on Y: \(CGFloat(acceleration.y))")
```

Now, run the game again. If you look at the console on the **Debug** area at the bottom of **Xcode**, you will see something that's similar to what's shown in the following screenshot:

```
acceleration on X:  0.1572265625
acceleration on Y: -0.779541015625
acceleration on X:  0.134262084960938
acceleration on Y: -0.775222778320312
acceleration on X:  0.0564422607421875
acceleration on Y: -0.774795532226562
acceleration on X: -0.0861968994140625
acceleration on Y:  0.788467407226562
acceleration on X: -0.150238037109375
acceleration on Y: -0.812240600585938
acceleration on X: -0.14544677734375
acceleration on Y: -0.823715209960938
acceleration on X: -0.0222930908203125
acceleration on Y: -0.816604614257812
acceleration on X:  0.013763427734375
acceleration on Y: -0.014544677734375
```

As you can see, while the acceleration on the *x* coordinate goes from `-0.2` to `0.2`, which corresponds to a slight slope to the left or right, the acceleration on the *y* coordinate is always `-0.7` or lower, which corresponds to the way we hold the device vertically.

We are going to take these values into account for the game movement to be more accurate and the player's position to be as comfortable as possible.

Compensating for the position of the device

To calibrate the position of the device, we will need to declare a new variable. So, add the following line at the top of the `GameScene` class:

```
private var initialAcceleration: CMAcceleration!
```

Let's initialize it once the accelerometer data is available. Replace the following lines in `useAccelerometerData`:

```
// Calculate next position on X coordinate
var nextPositionX: CGFloat = self.rabbit.position.x +
CGFloat(acceleration.x) * 1500.0 * CGFloat(deltaTime)
print("acceleration on X: \(CGFloat(acceleration.x))")
print("acceleration on Y: \(CGFloat(acceleration.y))")
```

Replace the preceding lines with the following ones:

```
// Getting initial acceleration
if self.initialAcceleration == nil {
    self.initialAcceleration =
self.motionManager.accelerometerData!.acceleration
}

// Calculate next position on X coordinate
var nextPositionX: CGFloat = self.rabbit.position.x +
CGFloat(acceleration.x - initialAcceleration.x) * 1500.0 *
CGFloat(deltaTime)
print("acceleration on X: \(CGFloat(acceleration.x -
initialAcceleration.x))")
print("acceleration on Y: \(CGFloat(acceleration.y -
initialAcceleration.y))")
```

With this code, we initialized the initial acceleration data if this has not been done. Then we used it to calculate the next position.

We also used the initial acceleration to show on the console the current acceleration. Execute the game now, and you will see that the acceleration values are lower and specifically, the *y* coordinate's acceleration is near 0.0, as shown in the following screenshot:

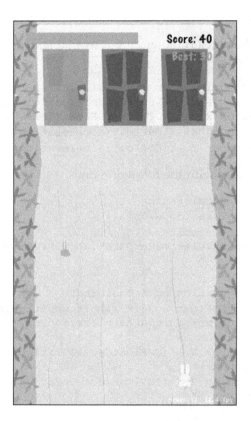

Adding shaders to our game

A shader or an instance of the SKShader class is an object that represents an **Open Graphics Library Embedded Systems (OpenGL ES)** or **(GLES)**. It is a fragment shader, which is an algorithm that modifies the drawing behavior of the node that it is applied to.

 Open Graphics Library (OpenGL) is an application programing interface that utilizes the **Graphics Processing Unit (GPU)** to render graphic elements.

You can use the effect shown in the following screenshot by applying shaders:

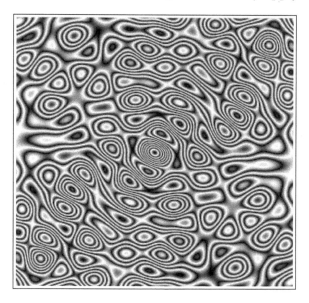

In order to apply a shader to a node, we need to create a SKShader instance from a fragment shader algorithm and assign it to the shader property of the desired object.

The shader creation and compilation takes a big amount of CPU memory. So that's why we need to keep in mind the following things:

- Avoid initializing shaders while the game is running; it's better to create them when the game is being launched

- Avoid modifying the algorithm source of the shader as it will recompile the shader, resulting in a loss of performance

- Reuse shaders when several nodes show the same behavior; you will avoid losing a big amount of memory

When developing the shader algorithm for iOS or Mac OS X, we can utilize the following variables:

- u_texture: A sampler associated with the texture that's used to render a node

- u_time: The elapsed time in a simulation

- u_sprite_size: The size of the sprite in pixels

- `u_path_length`: This variable can be used only when the shader is applied to the `strokeShader` property of an `SKShapeNode` class reference as it represents the length of the shape's path in points

- `v_tex_coord`: This is the point associated with the texture's access and by default, it references the (0.0, 0.0) point

- `v_color_mix`: A premultiplied color value for the node where the shader is being applied

- `v_path_distance`: This variable can only be used when the `shader` is applied to the `strokeShader` property of an `SKShapeNode` class reference as it represents the distance along the shape's path in points

When developing the `shader` algorithm, we need to have in mind that it should be wrapped in a `main()` function, which must set the `gl_FragColor` variable to a desired color.

We are going to use shaders to give the wrong doors a psychedelic look. So, let's start by declaring a new variable. Add the following line at the top of `GameScene`:

```
private var doorShader: SKShader!
```

This will represent the shader instance that we will share for every wrong door and which will appear on a wave.

Now, let's initialize this variable by calling a new method in `didMoveToView`. Add the following line to this method just before `self.initializeWall()`:

```
self.initializeShader()
```

Implement this using the following block of code:

```
func initializeShader() {
    // Initialize shaders
    self.doorShader = SKShader(fileNamed: "shader.fsh")
}
```

The preceding code is pretty easy; we are just creating a shader as a new instance of `SKShader` using a file called `shader.fsh` as the source, which is the file that contains the `shader` algorithm.

Let's add this new file to the project by performing the following steps:

1. Right-click on the **Resources** group in the project navigator and select **Add Files to InsideTheHat...**.

2. You'll find `shader.fsh` in the `7338_05_Resources` folder that had you previously unzipped. Select this file and click on **Add**.

If you open this file, you will see an algorithm that was developed using the **OpenGL ES 2.0** shading language and some of the variables that were previously mentioned. The algorithm was taken from `https://github.com/HeshamAmiri/SpriteKitShader`. It will create a psychedelic effect on the nodes where we it is applied.

So, now that we have the required source and the `shader` created, let's apply it to the doors. For this purpose, in `setDoorAttributes`, add the following lines at the end of the `if (arc4random_uniform(2) == 0) {` clause related to the left door:

```
// Set door shader
leftDoor.shader = self.doorShader
```

This will assign the new shader to the `shader` property of the left door.

As we don't want to apply the shader to the correct doors, add the following lines at the end of the `else` clause of the `if` statement:

```
// Remove shader
leftDoor.shader = nil
```

Let's add the same lines to the center and right doors respectively, as follows:

```
// Set door shader
centerDoor.shader = self.doorShader
```

For the center door, at the end of `if (arc4random_uniform(2) == 0) {`, add the following lines of code after the `else` block of the `if` statement:

```
// Remove shader
centerDoor.shader = nil
```

Finally, let's apply the same change for the right door. Add the following lines at the end of `if (arc4random_uniform(2) == 0) {` for the right door:

```
// Set door shader
rightDoor.shader = self.doorShader
```

Add the following ones at the end of its corresponding `else` clause:

```
// Remove shader
rightDoor.shader = nil
```

If you run the game now, you will see the new effect appearing on the doors, as shown in the following screenshot:

Turning on the lights

One of the most important elements in a game is lighting as it helps you give the desired atmosphere or highlight some places on the scene.

SpriteKit provides the `SKLightNode` class that gives us the capability of creating lights and treating them as nodes and, as a consequence of that, we can decide which nodes on the scene will interact with the lights, casting shadows.

It's important to take into account that even though lights are nodes, they have no visual representation unless we associate a `sprite` node to it. We also need to bear in mind that it's possible that the shadows produced by a source of light will be shown over other nodes.

When allowing a node to be affected by a source of light in the scene, there are three properties that we can use to define its behavior:

- `lightingBitMask`: Thanks to this property, the sprite will be affected by the light with specular, diffuse, and ambient light.

- `shadowCastBitMask`: Thanks to this property, a shadow will be created in the opposite direction of the light being rendered over the rest of the nodes with a `zPosition` lower than the previous node.

- `shadowedBitMask`: Thanks to this property, when a node intersects another node's shadow, if its `zPosition` is lower than that of the other node, it will be affected by the shadow. This property will modify how the nodes in the previous case are drawn.

We will use the lights to create a sun, illuminate the scene, and cast some shadows. For this purpose, we are going to learn how to create light in two ways. The first way involves the creation of light thanks to the `SpriteKit` editor that's available in `Xcode`. The second way involves programmatically creating it.

Creating lights with the editor

To create lights using the `SpriteKit` editor, we are going to create a scene file (an `.sks` file), to add light there and then build the rest of the game as we have been doing until now. The **SpriteKit** editor provides an easy and visual way of creating sprites, lights, physics, emitter nodes, actions, and other elements.

Let's start by creating this scene file by performing the following steps:

1. Right-click on **Resources**.
2. Select **New File...**.

3. Navigate to **iOS | Resource**. You will see a window that's similar to what's shown in the following screenshot:

4. Choose the **SpriteKit Scene** option and click on **Next**.
5. Call it `GameScene` and click on **Create**.

Now, open the file and add a new light, which can be found by selecting the **Light** option from the **Object library** to the right of **Xcode**:

Click on the **Light** option and drag it on the scene so that it is placed outside the view on the top-left corner, which is similar to what's shown in the following screenshot:

Now that the **Light** is placed in the scene, let's take a look to its properties, which will be found in the **Attributes inspector** to the right of **Xcode**.

As you can see, there are several properties, but we are going to focus on just some of them:

- Position: Thanks to this property, we can set the light where we want. I've chosen -65.8 and 1000.8 for the *x* and *y* coordinates respectively.

- z: This property makes a reference to the zPosition attribute of the light node. For the sake of this section, I've chosen 1.

- Color: This gives a reference to the light's color. I chose yellow and set the **Opacity** to 50%.

- Shadow Color: This gives a reference to the color of the shadow cast by the light. I chose black and set the **Opacity** to 50%.

- Ambient Color: This gives a reference to the ambient color of the light. I chose black and set the **Opacity** to 50% too.

- Falloff: This property gives a reference to how the light decays with distance. Its value is 1.0 by default, which means that it will decay linearly, but you can choose a positive value between 0.0 and 1.0. I've chosen 0.5.

- Enabled: This property corresponds to the enabled attribute of the light and indicates that the light affects the rest of the nodes in the scene. Its value is true by default (this can be checked in the editor). So let's leave it as it is.

- Lighting Mask: This property gives a reference to the lightingBitMask attribute. This value will set a mask so that the light will affect every node with the same mask. I chose 1.

Apart from these properties, we can modify an SKLightNode instance in the **SpriteKit** editor that has some other properties to highlight:

- shadowCastBitMask: If this mask corresponds to that of the light, the node will cast shadows that are affected by the corresponding light

- shadowedBitMask: This node is affected by the shadows that are cast by the sources of light with the same mask

Now that we have the lighting configured, we need to make some changes to the scenes.

Let's start by forcing our game to load the game scene when we initialize it on the main menu. In the initGame method of MenuScene, replace the following lines:

```
let gameScene = GameScene(size: view!.bounds.size)
self.view?.presentScene(gameScene, transition: sceneTransition)
```

Replace the preceding lines with the following lines of code:

```
let gameScene = GameScene(fileNamed: "GameScene")
gameScene?.size = view!.bounds.size
self.view?.presentScene(gameScene!, transition: sceneTransition)
```

This will take the GameScene.sks file to create the scene. We also specify the size, which will be the same as the one that was mentioned in the previous version of the scene to cover the entire view. Then, we present the scene using the same transition.

We need to make a couple of changes in GameScene too. So open it and add the following lines to the initializeEnemy method before addChild(enemy):

```
// Set puppet shadow masks
enemy.puppet.shadowCastBitMask = 1
enemy.puppet.shadowedBitMask = 1
```

We want just the puppet to be affected by the sunlight. So that's why, we set the same mask value as the ones that we entered for the light in the **SpriteKit** editor.

Now that the light and the enemy node are configured, let's test it on a physical device. If you run the game now, you will see something that's similar to what's shown in the following screenshot:

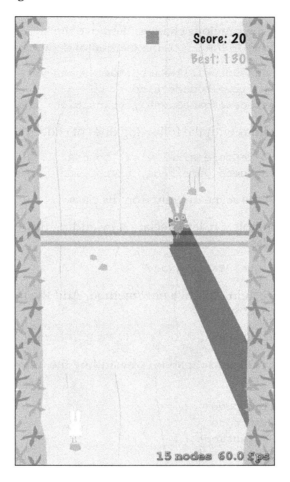

As you can see, the puppet casts a shadow that is produced by the sunlight, which will cover the full scene and it will appear as if the sun is setting. It's not possible to achieve a different result as it is a two-dimensional game. So, if we want to cast other types of shadows, we will need to create three-dimensional scenes using **SceneKit**, the 3D game engine that's provided by Apple Inc.

Programmatically creating lights

In this section, we are going to simulate the same effect that was achieved in the preceding section by creating a source of light with the same properties from scratch.

Let's start by reverting the previous changes. Remove the `GameScene.sks` file and replace the following lines in the `initGame` method of `MenuScene`:

```
let gameScene = GameScene(fileNamed:"GameScene")
gameScene?.size = view!.bounds.size
self.view?.presentScene(gameScene!, transition: sceneTransition)
```

Replace the preceding lines with the following lines of code:

```
let gameScene = GameScene(size: view!.bounds.size)
self.view?.presentScene(gameScene, transition: sceneTransition)
```

In this way, we created the scene directly from its class.

We will need a new variable. So, let's declare it by adding the following line at the top of the `GameScene` class:

```
private var sunLight: SKLightNode!
```

To initialize this, we are going to call a new method. Add the following line just at the beginning of `didMoveToView`:

```
self.initializeLightNode()
```

Implement `self.initializeLightNode()` by adding the following block of code within this method:

```
func initializeLightNode() {
    // Create light node
    sunLight = SKLightNode()

    // Set falloff value
    sunLight.falloff = 0.5

    // Set zPosition
    sunLight.zPosition = 1

    // Specify position
    sunLight.position = CGPoint(x: -65.8, y:1000.8)

    // Set ambient color
    sunLight.ambientColor = UIColor(red: 0.0, green: 0.0, blue:
0.0, alpha: 0.5)
```

```
    // Set light color
    sunLight.lightColor = UIColor(red: 0.0, green: 1.0, blue: 1.0,
    alpha: 0.5)

    // Set shadow color
    sunLight.shadowColor = UIColor(red: 0.0, green: 0.0, blue:
    0.0, alpha: 0.5)

    // Add light to the scene
    self.addChild(sunLight)
}
```

As you can see, we initialized the sunlight and then we set all the values as we specified in the previous section.

If you run the game now, you will face the same behavior that you previously encountered:

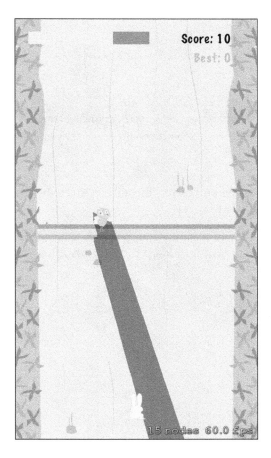

2-star challenge: moving lights

In this challenge, I want you to simulate the sun moving along the day so that you can see how we can treat lights as nodes. So, try to move the sun from left to right as the game moves forward.

Solution

To achieve this behavior, we are going to update the sun's position every time a wave finishes so that it will change gradually.

Let's start by calling a new method at the end of `initializeWave`:

```
// Update sun position
self.updateSunPosition()
```

Implement this using the following lines of code:

```
func updateSunPosition() {
    // Move sun on the x coordinates
    sunLight.position.x += 10.0

    // Reset sun position if needed
    if sunLight.position.x >= view!.bounds.size.width + 65.8 {
        sunLight.position.x = -65.8
    }
}
```

As you can see, we move the sun along the *x* coordinate by increasing its position by `10.0` every time a wave is initialized.

Also, we reset its position when `sunLight.position.x` achieves the last position on the right-hand side, as we want it to keep moving until the game is over.

If you run the game now, you will see how the sun moves now, as shown in the following screenshot:

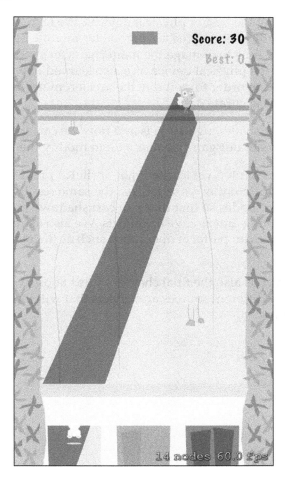

Summary

In this chapter, we learned several techniques that will help us create amazing visual effects by making the best of physical devices. We learned how to start receiving motion data by enabling the accelerometer module of the `motion` manager. Thanks to this, we saw how to manage the main character's movement using the accelerometer or position physical device. We also learned how to take into account the original orientation in order to calibrate the accelerometer/accelerometer-related information and obtain accurate data.

Then, we saw what the shader algorithm is and how we can apply the `Open GL` algorithms to the nodes of our game so that we can modify the way they are drawn.

Toward the end of the chapter, we learned that SpriteKit provides the capability of creating lights in two different ways to achieve the same results. Thanks to these lights, we can configure nodes so that they can cast shadows that are affected by the desired lights, creating amazing visual effects. We also learnt that lights can be treated as nodes and we can perform operations such as the modification of position on them.

The next chapter, which is also the final chapter of this book, will show us some skills to know how to create different sources and effects that will improve the quality of games and applications.

6
Auxiliary Techniques

The previous chapter explored the use of some techniques to squeeze the potential out of physical devices in order to control the main character's movement with an accelerometer or to create stunning visual effects thanks to **shaders**, lights, and shadows. This chapter will show us how to load and set up a particle system in order to create amazing effects such a fire, smog, and explosions.

We will also take advantage of SpriteKit animations to provide a dynamic look to the existing apps. Finally, we will learn how to find art and audio resources or even create our own audio and fonts using third-party tools.

We will explore the following topics in this chapter:

- How to load and set up a particle system
- How to add SpriteKit in apps
- Using third-party tools to create audio and fonts
- How to find art and audio that can be included in games

Creating particle systems

You probably don't know what a particle system is, but I'm sure that you have seen a lot of them. If you think about some sci-fi or action films that you may have watched of late, you will remember that they are plenty of special effects made by computers such as fire, explosions, smog, rain, and snow.

These effects have something in common; all of them are composed of hundreds of small components, or particles, that create the desired result by moving or changing the size or color of each particle independently.

In SpriteKit, we can easily create special effects, which are also known as particle systems, thanks to the SKEmitterNode class, which allows us to create and render small particle sprites to get the desired results.

On the other hand, SpriteKit provides a visual way of creating an emitter and editing its properties using the **Particle Emitter** editor that's included in **Xcode**. In the following sections, you are going to learn how to programmatically create an emitter node with the aforementioned editor .

Creating an emitter with the editor

In order to use the **Particle Emitter** editor, we need to create a SpriteKit file (an .sks file) by performing the following steps:

1. Unzip 7338_06_Resources.zip, where you will find InsideTheHat_init. zip. Unzip InsideTheHat_init.zip and open the project with **Xcode**.

2. Right-click on **Resources**.

3. Select **New File...**.

4. Select **iOS | Resource**, and you will see a screen that's similar to what's shown in the following screenshot:

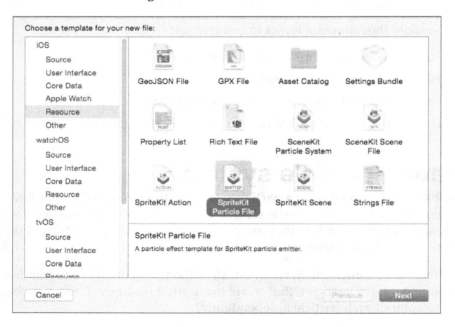

5. Choose **SpriteKit Particle File** and click on **Next**.

6. Choose **Snow** as **Particle template** and click on **Next**.

7. Name it `SnowParticle` and select where you want it to be saved before clicking on the **Create** button.

As you can see, if you look at the **Resources** group window, you will find that these steps have created two files, namely `spark.png` and `SnowParticle.sks`. If you now select the `SnowParticle.sks` file in the project navigator, it will be shown in the **Particle Emitter** editor, where you will see its default properties on the right-hand side. But first of all, touch the grey area at the center of the editor to see how the initial effect looks:

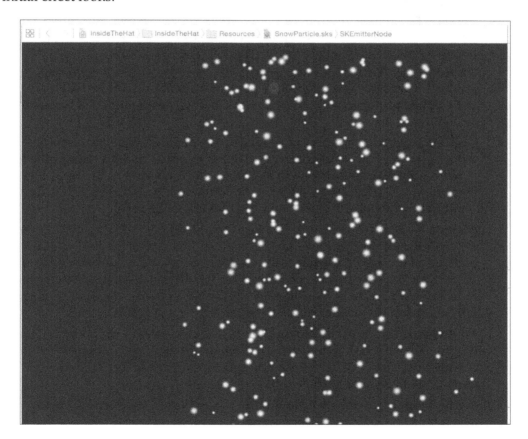

These properties are as follows:

- **Name**: This property makes a reference to the name attributes of the `SKEmitterNode` class and allows us identify the node so that it can be easily handled later.

- **Background**: This property allows us to set a background color to the emitter, but we can remove it by setting its opacity to 0.

- **Particles Birthrate**: This allows us to set the `particleBirthRate` property that indicates the rate at which the particles are emitted.

- **Particles Maximum**: This allows us to modify the `numParticlesToEmit` property that indicates the number of particles emitted before stopping the emission process. By default, the value is 0. This means that the emitter will endlessly generate particles. A positive value means that this number of particles will be created before stopping the emission process.

- **Lifetime Start**: This allows us to modify the `particleLifetime` property, which indicates the amount of time the particle will live. The default value in the editor for the snow is 8, while it is 0.0 if we programmatically create the emitter.

- **Lifetime Range**: This allows us to modify the `particleLifetimeRange` property, which allows us to specify a value that will be used to generate a random number between 0 and the property's value. Half of the resulting number will be randomly subtracted or added to the `particleLifetime` object to get the final lifetime value. The default value is 0.0.

- **Position Range**: This property allows us to modify `particlePositionRange`, which defines a maximum value that the x or y coordinates can randomly get. Half of this random value will be added to the original emitter's position to calculate the next particle position. The default value in the editor for the snow is 363.44 for the x coordinate and 5 for the y coordinate, while it is (0.0, 0.0) if we programmatically create the emitter.

- **Angle Start**: This allows us to modify the `emissionAngle` property, which specifies the direction in degrees in which the particles are emitted. The default value in the editor for the snow is 269.863, while it is 0.0 if we programmatically create the emitter.

- **Angle Range**: This allows us to modify the `emissionAngleRange` object, which indicates the maximum number of degrees the initial angle added to half of a random value between 0 and the specified range will vary. The default value in the editor for the snow is -22.918, while it is 0.0 if we programmatically create the emitter.

- **Speed Start**: This property allows us to modify the `particleSpeed` property, which specifies the base speed in points per second with which the particles are emitted. The default value in the editor for the snow is 80, while it is 0.0 if we programmatically create the emitter.

- **Speed Range**: This allows us to modify the `particleSpeedRange` property, which specifies a maximum range that a random value will take. Half of this random value is added to the particle's speed to get the resultant final speed. The default value in the editor for the snow is 100, while it is 0.0 if we programmatically create the emitter, which means that all the particles move at the same speed.

- **Acceleration**: This allows us to modify the `xAcceleration` and the `yAcceleration` properties, which will apply a horizontal and vertical acceleration to each coordinate's velocity respectively. The default value in the editor for the snow is 0 and -10, while it is 0.0 for both x and y if we programmatically create the emitter.

- **Alpha Start**: This allows us to modify the initial alpha property of the emitted particles. The default value for the snow is 1.0 if you create it either by using the editor or programmatically.

- **Alpha Range**: This allows us to modify the `particleColorAlphaRange` property, which defines a range of values that will randomly modify the initial alpha value. The default value in the editor for the snow is 0.2, while it is 0.0 if we create the emitter programmatically.

- **Alpha Speed**: This allows us to modify the `particleColorAlphaSpeed` property, which indicates the rate at which the alpha component of a particles' color changes per second. The default value for the snow is 0.0 if you create it either by using the editor or programmatically.

- **Scale Start**: This allows us to modify the `particleScale` property, which determines how large a particle is when it is created. The default value in the editor for the snow is 0.2, while it is 1.0 if we create the emitter programmatically, which means that the particle size will be the same as the image used to generate it.

- **Scale Range**: This allows us to modify the `particleScaleRange` property, which determines an amount the size of the particle can vary as compared to the initial size. The default value in the editor for the snow is 0.2, while it is 0.0 if we create the emitter programmatically.

- **Scale Speed**: This allows us to modify the `particleScaleSpeed` property, which indicates the rate at which the scale of the particles changes per second. The default value for the snow is 0.0 if you create it either by using the editor or programmatically.

- **Rotation Start**: This allows us to modify the `particleRotation` property, which determines an initial rotation angle in radians for each particle. The default value for the snow is 0.0 in both the editor and if you're doing it programmatically.

- **Rotation Range**: This allows us to modify the `particleRotationRange` property, which determines the amount that the rotation of the particle can vary from the initial stage. The default value for the snow is 0.0 for both the editor as well as if it's being done programmatically.

- **Rotation Speed**: This allows us to modify the `particleRotationSpeed` property, which indicates the speed at which a particle rotates, and is expressed in radians per second. The default value for the snow is 0.0 for both the editor and if it's being done programmatically.

- **Color Blend Factor**: This allows us to modify the `particleColorBlendFactor` property, which determines the average starting value for the particle's color. The default value in the editor for the snow is 1.0, while it is 0.0 if we create the emitter programmatically.

- **Color Blend Range**: This allows us to modify the `particleColorBlendFactorRange` property, which determines an amount by which the blend of the particle can vary from the initial one. The default value for the snow is 0.0 if we create it either by using the editor or programmatically.

- **Color Blend Speed**: This allows us to modify the `particleColorBlendFactorSpeed` property, which indicates the speed at which a particle's color is blended, and it is expressed in seconds. The default value for the snow is 0.0 for both the editor and if you create it programmatically.

- **Color Ramp**: This allows us to choose the color that's used to blend the particle's color.

- **Blend Mode**: This allows us to modify the `particleBlendMode` property, which can get one of the following seven values:

  ○ **Alpha**: The source and destination colors are blended by multiplying the source alpha value. This is the default value for both the editor and if you're creating it programmatically, for example, `SKBlendMode.SKBlendModeAlpha`.

  ○ **Add**: The source and destination colors are added together. If we want to set it programmatically, we need to specify `SKBlendMode.SKBlendModeAdd`.

- ° **Subtract**: The source color is subtracted from the destination color. If we want to set it programmatically, we need to specify `SKBlendMode.SKBlendModeSubtract`.

- ° **Multiply**: The source color is multiplied by the destination color. If we want to set it programmatically, we need to specify `SKBlendMode.SKBlendModeMultiply`.

- ° **MultiplyX2**: The source color is multiplied by the destination color and then doubled. If we want to set it programmatically, we need to specify `SKBlendMode.SKBlendModeMultiplyX2`.

- ° **Screen**: The source color is added to the destination color times the inverted source color. If we want to set it programmatically, we need to specify `SKBlendMode.SKBlendModeScreen`.

- ° **Replace**: The source color replaces the destination color. If we want to set it programmatically, we need to specify `SKBlendMode.SKBlendModeReplace`.

- **Field Mask**: This allows us to modify the `fieldBitMask` property that determines which categories of the physics fields can interact with the particles. The default value for the snow is 0.0 for both the editor and if you're creating it programmatically.

- **Custom Shader**: This allows us to modify the `shader` property, which helps us specify an Open GL algorithm in order to modify the color of the particles emitted. The default value for the snow is `nil` for both the editor and if you're creating it programmatically.

These are the most important properties of a particle system and, as you can see, when we create an emitter using the editor, it will be initialized with different values for its properties, depending on the type of emitter that we have selected.

We are going to take advantage of the default values to generate the first particles system. Let's add some code to the project.

We will need a new variable. So, let's add the following declaration at the top of `GameScene.swift`:

```
private var emitterNode: SKEmitterNode!
```

In order to initialize this, we will call a new method. Add the following line to `didMoveToView` just before `initializeLifeBar`:

```
self.initializeEmitterNode()
```

Implement this using the following block of code:

```
func initializeEmitterNode() {
    // Initialize emitter
    emitterNode = SKEmitterNode(fileNamed: "SnowParticle")

    // Add emitter to the scene
    addChild(emitterNode)
}
```

With this method, we initialize the emitter using the `SnowParticle.sks` file that we previously created. Then, we add it to the scene.

If you run the game now, you will see how the emitter looks with its default values:

There is a problem that we could have previewed. The default position of the emitter is placed at the bottom of the scene and it is barely visible (you can see only a part of a snow fleck in the following screenshot) because its original y coordinate value is 5:

We are going to fix this quickly. You just need to make a couple of modifications in the SnowParticle.sks file:

1. Set **Position Range X** to **600**. Thus, the snow flakes will cover almost the entire width of an iPhone 6 device.

2. Set **Position Range Y** to **1800**. Thus, it will cover almost the entire height of an iPhone 6 device.

If you look closely, there is an issue with the current configuration of the emitter. The flecks' zPosition object is not correct and they appear below some elements of the scene and the result is weird.

However, before fixing this, let's make a couple of changes to the emitter file in order to adapt the snow's behavior to a stronger snowfall, as follows:

1. Set **Particles Birthrate** to **80**. Thus, we simulate that the snowfall is stronger than the default one.

2. Set **Lifetime Start** to **4**. This property, in collaboration with the previous change, will let us achieve the expected effect.

Then, in `GameScene`, add the following lines to the `initializeEmitterNode` method of the `GameScene` class just before `addChild(emitterNode)`:

```
// Specify zPosition
emitterNode.zPosition = 5
```

Run the game again and look at the final result, as shown in the following screenshot:

Creating the emitter programmatically

In the previous section, we saw how to load a particle system thanks to the visual editor provided by **Xcode**, but we faced a problem. The `GameScene.swift` is a static file and we cannot modify its behavior along the game's lifetime. However, if we create it programmatically, we can adjust it whenever we want.

In addition to this, we can also manipulate other properties such as `position` or `zPosition` that are usually handled in every game (and in our game specifically). So, in this section, we are going to manage the emitter programmatically.

Open `GameScene.swift` and add the following lines to the `initializeEmitterNode` method just before `emitterNode.zPosition = 5`:

```
emitterNode.particleBirthRate = 80.0
emitterNode.particleLifetime = 4.0
emitterNode.position = CGPoint(x: (view!.bounds.size.width/2), y:
```

```
view!.bounds.size.height)
emitterNode.particlePositionRange.dx = 600
emitterNode.particlePositionRange.dy = 1800
emitterNode.emissionAngle = 269.863
emitterNode.emissionAngleRange = -22.918
emitterNode.particleSpeed = 80.0
emitterNode.particleSpeedRange = 100.0
emitterNode.yAcceleration = -10.0
emitterNode.particleColorAlphaRange = 0.2
emitterNode.particleScale = 0.2
emitterNode.particleScaleRange = 0.2
emitterNode.particleColorBlendFactor = 1.0
```

As you can see, we are still using the file created with Xcode, but we are using it to modify some needed properties, such as the position, which will allow us to place the emitter at the center of any device no matter what its resolution is.

The rest of the properties have been assigned to match the values that we set in the file. Therefore, if you now run the game on any device, it will show the same behavior as what was created in the previous section. The output is as follows:

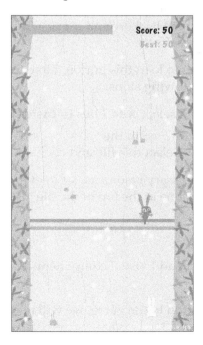

Combining SpriteKit and UIKit

As SpriteKit and **User Interface Kit** (**UIKit**) are frameworks that are available in iOS, we can expect to combine them in different ways. Actually, we can create games with SpriteKit and include components from UIKit and, on the other hand, we can create applications that show the elements that were created with SpriteKit.

These features give us great power and versatility, as we can join the capabilities provided by both the frameworks to create robust games or give a more dynamic look to existing applications.

In the following lines, we are going to learn how to use UIKit with SpriteKit and vice versa. So let's start by adding some element from UIKit into the game.

Including UIKit in a game

As you may already know, if you have tried to create an iOS application before, UIKit is a framework that provides all the components that are necessary to create an app.

In this section, we will harness the potential provided by UIKit to add a button into the game so that we can stop the background music that's playing or restart it, and we will also silence the sound effects.

We are going to use an image to load this button. First, let's add it to the game. For this purpose, perform the following steps:

1. Right-click on **Art** and select **Add Files to InsideTheHat…**.
2. You'll find `soundOffOn.png` in the `7338_06_Resources` folder that you previously unzipped. Select this file and click on **Add**.

Now that we have all the necessary resources, let's get to work. Open `GameScene.swift` and add the following line at the top of the file just after `import AVFoundation`:

```
import UIKit
```

Thus, we have the potential to add visual components (UIKit is the acronym for **User Interface Kit**) to the game.

As we are going to add a button to the game, we will need to declare a new variable. So, add the following line just after `private var emitterNode: SKEmitterNode!`:

```
private var soundOffOnButton: UIButton!
```

We have declared this variable as a UIButton object, which is the class provided by UIKit to create buttons on the touch screen.

> In this book, we are not going to get into the details of any UIKit component, but you can take a look at its framework reference webpage, which can be viewed by visiting https://developer.apple.com/library/ios/documentation/UIKit/Reference/UIKit_Framework.

The next step is to initialize this new variable. So, let's add the following method call at the end of the didMoveToView method:

```
self.initializeSoundOffOnButton()
```

Implement this using the following block of code:

```
func initializeSoundOffOnButton() {
    // Initialize UIButton
    soundOffOnButton = UIButton(frame: CGRectMake(view!.bounds.size.
width - rabbit.frame.width, view!.bounds.size.height - rabbit.frame.
width, rabbit.frame.width, rabbit.frame.width))

    // Set image to button
    soundOffOnButton.setImage(UIImage(named: "soundOffOn"), forState:
UIControlState.Normal)

    // Specify function to trigger
    soundOffOnButton.addTarget(self, action: "alternateSound",
forControlEvents: UIControlEvents.TouchUpInside)

    // Add button to view
    self.view!.addSubview(soundOffOnButton)
}
```

As you can see, we first initialized the UIButton, specifying a frame (a CGRectMake instance), by providing its initial position in the *x* and *y* coordinates, width, and height.

> Note how we are taking into account the rabbit size, as we don't want the button to be bigger than the main character.

Then, we specify the image that we want to use to render the button, and we specify the one that we had previously added to the project.

The button needs to know the action that it should trigger when it is touched, and this information needs to be provided by using the `addTarget` method of the class. This method allows us to specify the class (`self`) where the method (`alternateSound`) will be triggered when the desired event (`TouchUpInside`) happens. In this way, the button will execute what we expected.

Finally, we add the button to the scene. But if you pay attention, you will see that we are not adding the element as we have been doing previously using the `addChild` method; we are adding it as a sub-view of the scene's view.

In this way, we can't specify the `zPosition` value, but we will have complete control over the position that each component takes, as it will depend on the view that they are the children of.

Now that we have created the button, we just need to implement the method that we want to trigger when it is touched. But first, let's add a new variable that we will use to know whether the sound should be played or not:

```
private var isSoundOn: Bool = true
```

We create a Boolean flag that's initialized to `true` so that the game will start playing once the game begins. Now, add the following lines at the end of `GameScene` to implement the method that does the magic:

```
func alternateSound() {
    if isSoundOn {
        // Stop background music
        isSoundOn = false
        backgroundMusic.stop()
    } else {
        // Restart background music
        isSoundOn = true
        backgroundMusic.play()
    }
}
```

If the music is playing (the flag is `true`), we update its value and stop the background music. If it is not playing, we update the flag and restart the music.

This code will just stop the background music, but we also want the sound effects to stop. Therefore, we just need a last change. Replace the `playWrongDoorSound` and `playCorrectDoorSound` methods with the following ones:

```
func playWrongDoorSound() {
    if isSoundOn {
        // Play wrong door sound
```

```
        wrongDoorSound.play()
    }
}

func playCorrectDoorSound() {
    if isSoundOn {
        // Play correct door sound
        correctDoorSound.play()
    }
}
```

As you can see, we just check the flag in order to know whether the sounds must be played when the rabbit collides with some door or the enemies.

If you run the game now, you will see how this new button that was created with UIKit works:

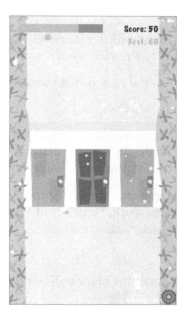

Including SpriteKit in an app

We have seen that we can incorporate UIKit elements into our games easily. Now, we are going to discover how we can use SpriteKit to create dynamic and visually attractive applications.

For this purpose, we are going to add some cloud nodes into an existing weather application and apply some actions to these nodes so that they will move from right to left.

First of all, we need to open the existing application by performing the following steps:

1. Unzip the `SpriteKitApp_init.zip` project that you will find in `7338_06_Resources`.

2. Open the `SpriteKitApp` file with **Xcode**.

If you look at the contents of this project, you will see that it has the appearance of a Single View application project, where you will find the following three important components:

- A **Resources** group with a `clouds.png` file will be present, which will be used to render some sprites on the app.

- A **Main.storyboard** that contains a view with one button and text field will also be seen. If you look at the **Connections inspector** to the right of **Xcode**, you will realize that the view (`Scene View`) is already connected to some outlet.

- The `ViewController.swift` file contains an `@IBOutlet` variable, which is the one that's connected to the view on the storyboard.

The most important thing here is the new outlet variable:

```
@IBOutlet var sceneView: SKView!
```

As you can see, it is a `SKView` variable, and it is currently raising a `Use of undeclared type 'SKView'` error. The reason behind why this warning is seen is that `SKView` is a class from SpriteKit, but we haven't imported it into the project.

So, the first thing that we need in order to include the SpriteKit elements into the application is to import this framework. Hence, add the following line at the top of `ViewController.swift` just after `import UIKit`:

```
import SpriteKit
```

Thanks to the previous line of code, the error will not be raised after this.

To show the sprites, we are going to create a scene that will be shown in the existing `sceneView` view. So for this purpose, we will need a new variable. Add the following line just after the declaration of `sceneView`:

```
private var scene: SKScene!
```

We have declared this scene as we usually do on a game. So now it's time to initialize it. For this purpose, we are going to call a new method. Add the following line of code at the end of the `viewDidLoad` method:

```
self.initializeScene()
```

Let's implement this method using the following block of code:

```
func initializeScene() {
    // Initialize scene
    scene = SKScene(size: view!.bounds.size)
    scene.backgroundColor = UIColor.whiteColor()

    // Add scene to view
    sceneView.presentScene(scene)
}
```

We initialized the scene using the size of the view, we set the background color to white and then we presented the scene in the view that we have linked to the storyboard component.

At this point, we have the application ready to host a game or the components that we want to add from SpriteKit. So, it's time for us to create the desired clouds. Add the following line of code towards the end of `viewDidLoad`:

```
self.initializeClouds()
```

Implement this using the following lines:

```
func initializeClouds() {
    // Random number of clouds to generate
    let numClouds = arc4random_uniform(10) + UInt32(15)
    for _ in 0...numClouds {
        // Initialize cloud node
        let clouds = SKSpriteNode(imageNamed: "clouds")
        clouds.alpha = 0.7

        // Random Y position
        let positionY = arc4random_uniform(UInt32(view!.bounds.size.
height))

        // Positioning the clouds
        clouds.position = CGPoint(x:view!.bounds.size.width + clouds.
size.width/2  , y: CGFloat(positionY))

        // Add clouds to scene
        scene.addChild(clouds)

        // Run actions on each node
        self.runCloudsAction(clouds)
    }
}
```

In this method, we created a random number of clouds between 15 and 24, as we create a random number between 0 and 9 and add 15 to this result. Then, we created each cloud using a `for` loop, where we first initialized a sprite node using the image file, and then we set its `alpha` property to 0.7 to give it a volatile look.

We want each cloud to be placed at a random height. Therefore, we created `positionY` as a random value of the entire view height and used it to initially place the cloud on the right-hand side of the screen and outside the view.

Finally, we added the sprite to the scene and called a new method, where we configured the actions that we want each node to execute. Add the following block of code to know what this method does:

```
func runCloudsAction(node: SKSpriteNode) {
    var moveAction:SKAction!
    var nextPosition: CGPoint

    // Setting the next position
    nextPosition = CGPoint(x: -node.size.width/2, y: node.position.y)

    // Move the clouds to the left side of the screen
    moveAction = SKAction.moveToX(nextPosition.x, duration:
Double(arc4random_uniform(8) + UInt32(4)))
}
```

We want the clouds to move from right to left. Therefore, we declare an `SKAction` variable and a point that will be the final point that the cloud will reach.

We specified this point so that it is the same as its initial place but on the opposite side of the screen. Then, we created the `movement` action as a `moveToX` object, where we indicated the position and a random duration that will be a random value between 4 and 11.

This method is incomplete. So, add the following lines at the end of `runCloudsAction` to give it the entire behavior:

```
// Reset the clouds position
let resetPositionAction = SKAction.runBlock {

// Random Y position
let positionY = arc4random_uniform(UInt32(self.view!.bounds.size.
height))

// Positioning the clouds
node.position = CGPoint(x:(self.view!.bounds.size.width + node.size.
width/2), y: CGFloat(positionY))
```

```
}

// Creating a delay action
let delayAction = SKAction.waitForDuration(1.0)
let sequence = SKAction.sequence([delayAction, moveAction,
resetPositionAction, delayAction])

// Runaction
node.runAction(SKAction.repeatActionForever(sequence))
```

In this block, we created a `runBlock` action, where we reset the cloud position by creating a `y` coordinate randomly. Then, we created a delay of 1 second in action and configured a sequence with the delay and the rest of the actions. Finally, we run the action in the node. So, let's execute the game now and check out what we have done:

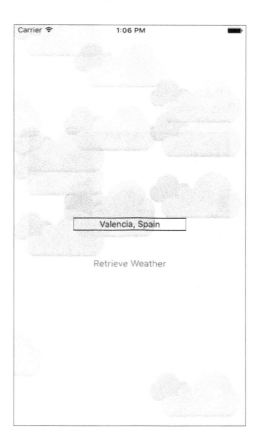

So that's how we can combine both the frameworks that are available in iOS to create powerful games and highly engaging applications.

Using third-party tools

In the following pages, we are going to see how we can use some tools to create audio resources. In addition to this, this section will show you how to make use of other complementary tools that are being provided by third-party companies or persons to create and use our own customized fonts.

Creating audio resources

Sounds and music is one of the most important elements in video games and usually, we as developers need to add some of these resources to our games. Usually, we also don't have enough budget to hire either audio composers or recording studios, and we need to take matters into our own hands.

I will show you the tools that we have at our disposal for this purpose and how we can use them to create audio resources.

Voice memos

This app is one of the apps that was integrated with iOS. Therefore, you will have it if you own an iPhone or iPad device:

You can use this utility to record short effects or sounds that can be exported in an .m4a file to a computer and played in SpriteKit games. In addition to this, this app allows us to perform this task easily, as you just need to push the **Record** and **Stop** buttons and then use the **Share** button.

For example, I used this app to record the sounds that we produce when the rabbit collides with a wrong or a correct door and then, I converted the file type.

 If you have no iOS device, you can record any audio with another application that's available in your phone or computer.

Audacity

Once I recorded the sound effects, I sent them to my computer and opened them with Audacity (for more information, visit http://sourceforge.net/projects/audacity), an open source software that's used to record and edit audio files.

I used this software to cut the part of the recorded file that I wanted and ignore the noise from the beginning and the end. Then, I exported the file to .mp3 for a better compression:

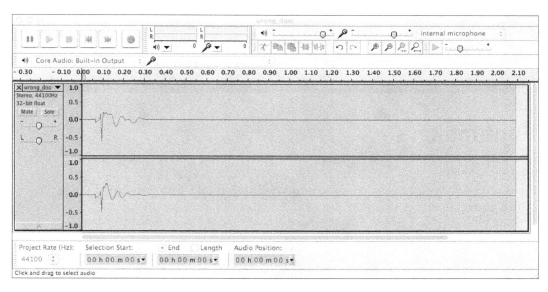

This tool also allows us to record sounds using the internal microphone from a computer or an external sound card and to perform a complete set of transformations, apply effects, and combine several tracks.

GarageBand

GarageBand is a software that is pre-installed with Mac OS X. It is a very powerful tool that's used to create professional musical productions. It has a battery of prerecorded audio pieces of a wide variety of instruments that I combined to create the background music that we can listen to in `InsideTheHat`.

In addition to this, GarageBand provides powerful tools and techniques that will allow you to create professional songs:

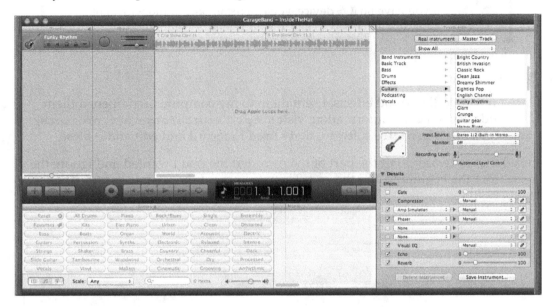

Font makers

There are several ways to create our own custom fonts; you will realize this when you visit `http://superdevresources.com/create-your-own-font`. I will not show you how to create you own font, but I'll show you how to use it into your game.

First, let's add the font that I've created thanks to `http://www.pentacom.jp/pentacom/bitfontmaker2`:

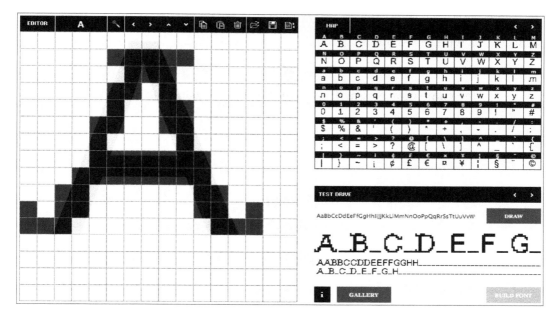

Perform the following steps:

1. In `InsideTheHat`, right-click on **Resources** and select **Add Files to InsideTheHat...**.

2. You'll find `customFont.ttf` in the `7338_06_Resources` folder that you previously unzipped. Select this file and click on **Add**.

Then, we need to know the project to which we are going to provide external fonts to the project. To know this, perform the following steps:

1. Select the `Info.plist` file in the project navigator.

2. Add a new **Array** key for **Fonts** provided by application.

3. For the **Item 0** key, specify the `customFont.ttf` value.

4. Ensure that the file is included in the build by checking whether it is specified in the **Copy Bundle Resources** directory inside the **Build Phases** section of the target configuration.

Finally, we need to specify this font when we create a label. So go to `MenuScene.swift` and replace the following line of code:

```
labelInitGame = SKLabelNode(fontNamed:"Arial Bold")
```

Replace this with the following line:

```
labelInitGame = SKLabelNode(fontNamed:"customFont")
```

If you run the game now, you will see that the game is using the new font:

How to find audio files

There are several websites where you will find audio resources of different types and licenses. Some of them are listed here:

- `http://soundbible.com`: This site offers a wide variety of sound bites, sound clips, and sound effects with different license types such as **Public Domain, Attribution 3.0, Attr-Noncommercial 3.0, Sampling Plus 1.0,** and **Noncommercial 3.0.**

- `http://www.partnersinrhyme.com`: This website has an interesting database of free sound effects, music, videos, **MIDI** files. It also provides collections of paid music of different genres of music.

- `http://www.pacdv.com/sounds`: Even though this site contains a short database of files, it provides high-quality, free, and very useful resources.

- `http://www.freesound.org`: This site contains a variety of Public Domain, Attribution, and Attribution Non-Commercial licensed audio resources. Here, you will also find a very active forum with information on how to create your own audio, sample requests, or even legal information.

- `http://www.royaltyfreemusicradio.com`: If you need radio station samples, you can find several resources here. But you will need to pay to get some of their files.

- `http://www.musicloops.com`: This place contains a wide variety of free and paid high-quality and royalty-free audios.

- `http://www.freesoundeffects.com`: This site contains a very wide variety of professional and free sound effects.

- `http://www.naturemusicdownload.com`: If you need ambient music or sounds based on nature, this is your site. You need to pay to use the content that's available here.

- `http://audiojungle.net`: Here, you will find lots of professional, paid content to provide sound for your apps and games.

The following screenshot shows one of the website from you can get free or premium audio files:

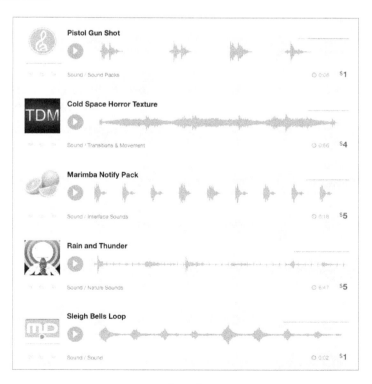

How to find images

You will find a lot of images that can be used in your games at the following links:

- `http://opengameart.org`: This site provides free 2D and 3D art, concept art, and textures that can be used in our games.

- `http://www.rpg-palace.com`: If you are developing an RPG game, this is your place. Here, you will find free characters, scenarios, and other related resources to create your game.

- `http://untamed.wild-refuge.net/rmxpresources.php?characters`: Like the previous site, you will find a variety of free resources for your RPG games here.

- `http://www.textures.com`: This place is recommended if you wish to find a wide variety of free textures that you can use in your games.

- `http://www.spiralgraphics.biz/packs/browse.htm`: This is yet another complete site that can be used to find high-quality and free textures.

- `http://www.pixelresort.com/blog/app-icon-template`: This site offers a template to generate all the icons for your game, which can be uploaded to the App Store.

- `http://qvectors.net`: This site provides high-quality, free, and paid vector resources.

- `http://www.gameartguppy.com`: On this site, you will find a wide variety of amazing paid sprites for your games.

- `http://www.gameart2d.com/freebies.html`: An amazing collection of animated sprites, icons, and beautiful backgrounds can be found here.

- `http://unluckystudio.com`: This is another site with amazing assets related to free art and images.

- `http://www.graphic-buffet.com/freebies`: A wide variety of images can be found here.

- `http://gameartpartners.com`: Amazing free resources can be found here.

The following screenshot shows one of the website from you can get free or premium game images:

Summary

In this final chapter of the book, we learned some techniques that can be used to create amazing visual results that are similar to the special effects in films. For this purpose, we had a look at how we can create particle systems, either by using the editor available in Xcode, or programmatically so that we can modify its properties to improve our game performance.

We learned how to combine SpriteKit and UIKit to make use of the potential that game elements have in applications. Vice versa, we also learned how to use typical app elements to create robust games.

In the last half of the chapter, we developed some skills so that we can create our own audio resources and customized text fonts. We had a look at some places where we can find free and paid music files on the Internet that can be included in our games. Finally, we had a look at where we can find amazing visual content, such as sprites, textures, backgrounds, and visual elements, on different websites.

Index

A

accelerometer
  CMMotionManager class 154-158
  device position, compensating 159
  using 153, 154
animations
  creating, in SpriteKit 101-103
Audacity
  URL 195
audio files
  finding 198, 199
  references 198
audio resources
  Audacity 195
  creating 194
  GarageBand 196
  voice memos 194, 195
AVFoundation 68, 69

C

CMMotionManager class 154-158
collision management
  about 55
  collisions 55
  collisions, handling 55-58
collisions
  checking 58, 59
collisions, animating
  about 104
  solution 105, 106

D

data
  loading 140
  saving 140

E

editor
  lights, creating with 165-169
emitter
  properties 178-181

F

font makers
  references 196, 197

G

game
  ending 113-116
  restarting 117
  shaders, adding to 160-163
  solution 117-120
game engines
  defining 1
game loop
  about 19
  URL 19
geometrical primitives 107-111
GLES 160
Graphics Processing Unit (GPU) 160

R

RGBA (Red, Blue, Green, and Alpha)
    color 22

S

scene graph 14
scene hierarchy 14
scenes
    and transitions 124
screen resolutions
    working with 31, 32
shader algorithm
    variables 161
shaders
    about 175
    adding, to game 160-163
    using 153
SKLabelNode class 64
SKNode class
    custom class behavior, handling 82-90
    defining 14
    extending 75-77
    new class, creating 77-81
    properties 15
    used, for organizing scene 17, 18
SKScene class
    defining 18
    game loop 19, 20
    properties 20
SKShader
    references 163
SKSpritenode and EnemyType variables
    references 79
SKSpriteNode class
    defining 24-27
    URL 23
SKTransition class
    about 124-127
    methods, defining 124, 125
sound effects
    reproducing 69-71
SpriteKit
    about 2
    and UIKit, combining 186

animations, creating 101-103
    including, in app 189-193
SpriteKit class
    URL 14
SpriteKit project
    creating 2-5
    default project, displaying 7-13
    running 6

T

texture atlases 101
third-party tools
    audio resources, creating 194
    font makers 196, 197
    using 194
touchesBegan method 36
touchesCancelled method 36
touchesEnded method 36
touchesMoved method 36
touch events
    actions, handling 40
    handling 35-40
    running, through doors 42-45
    wall, building 41
transitions
    and scenes 124
tutorial
    completing 144
    creating 128-130
    property list files 146-149
    solution 144, 145
tutorial steps
    updating 132-140

U

User Interface Kit (UIKit)
    about 186
    and SpriteKit, combining 186
    including, into game 186-188
    URL 187

X

Xcode
    URL 2

Thank you for buying
Getting Started with SpriteKit

About Packt Publishing

Packt, pronounced 'packed', published its first book, *Mastering phpMyAdmin for Effective MySQL Management*, in April 2004, and subsequently continued to specialize in publishing highly focused books on specific technologies and solutions.

Our books and publications share the experiences of your fellow IT professionals in adapting and customizing today's systems, applications, and frameworks. Our solution-based books give you the knowledge and power to customize the software and technologies you're using to get the job done. Packt books are more specific and less general than the IT books you have seen in the past. Our unique business model allows us to bring you more focused information, giving you more of what you need to know, and less of what you don't.

Packt is a modern yet unique publishing company that focuses on producing quality, cutting-edge books for communities of developers, administrators, and newbies alike. For more information, please visit our website at www.packtpub.com.

About Packt Open Source

In 2010, Packt launched two new brands, Packt Open Source and Packt Enterprise, in order to continue its focus on specialization. This book is part of the Packt Open Source brand, home to books published on software built around open source licenses, and offering information to anybody from advanced developers to budding web designers. The Open Source brand also runs Packt's Open Source Royalty Scheme, by which Packt gives a royalty to each open source project about whose software a book is sold.

Writing for Packt

We welcome all inquiries from people who are interested in authoring. Book proposals should be sent to author@packtpub.com. If your book idea is still at an early stage and you would like to discuss it first before writing a formal book proposal, then please contact us; one of our commissioning editors will get in touch with you.

We're not just looking for published authors; if you have strong technical skills but no writing experience, our experienced editors can help you develop a writing career, or simply get some additional reward for your expertise.

Swift by Example

ISBN: 978-1-78528-470-0   Paperback: 284 pages

Create funky, impressive applications using Swift

1. Learn Swift language features quickly, with playgrounds and in-depth examples.

2. Implement real iOS apps using Swift and Cocoapods.

3. Create professional video games with SpriteKit, SceneKit, and Swift.

Learning iOS 8 Game Development Using Swift

ISBN: 978-1-78439-355-7   Paperback: 366 pages

Create robust and spectacular 2D and 3D games from scratch using Swift – Apple's latest and easy-to-learn programming language

1. Create engaging games from the ground up using SpriteKit and SceneKit.

2. Boost your game's visual performance using Metal - Apple's new graphics library.

3. A step-by-step approach to exploring the world of game development using Swift.

Please check **www.PacktPub.com** for information on our titles